OVER THE EDGE

Larry Vardiman
Phil. 2:13

851 Vista Dr
Camano, Wa. 98282
360-572-4005

OVER THE EDGE

LARRY VARDIMAN

First printing: August 1999

ISBN: 0-89051-323-6
Library of Congress: 99-66476

Cover by Janell Robertson

Illustrations on pages 15, 24, and 51 are by Marvin Ross. All other illustrations are by Jonathan Chong.

Printed in the United States of America

ACKNOWLEDGMENTS AND DEDICATION

Many creationist organizations and individuals have conducted trips to the Grand Canyon because of its incredible significance in understanding the Genesis flood. During the 1960s and 1970s Drs. Ed Nafziger and Bernard Northrup of the Bible Science Association guided many groups into the canyon. Dr. Gary Parker of Answers in Genesis and David Coppedge of Creation Safaris have also taken groups of people to the canyon over the years before and after the Institute for Creation Research (ICR) began conducting tours. ICR was not the first, nor will it likely be the last, to expose people to the truth revealed in the rocks at the Grand Canyon.

Dr. Steve Austin should be given credit for the vision to initiate the first ICR Grand Canyon trip which led to the successful tours we have today. Somehow, Steve seems to have escaped being the butt of most of the humorous episodes in this book, but I suspect it was primarily because I didn't happen to be with him when an embarrassing event happened. Maybe next year.

I dedicate this book to my daughter Kelly, who backpacked with me several times when she was young and once on an ICR trip to the Grand Canyon. I believe her experience backpacking in the canyon may have contributed to her decision to enter the U.S. Air Force and complete technical school to become a security policeman. She provided security for an intelligence base in Germany and, for several months, for pilots in Saudi Arabia. I still have difficulty imagining her carrying an M-16 rifle and driving a Humvee, but I am proud of my daughter and what she has accomplished. I hope she enjoys this book as much as I enjoyed writing it.

My reviewers were Walter Barnhart, Kenneth Cumming, Hanna Rush, David McQueen, John Morris, Andrew Snelling, Steve Tecklenberg, Mary Thomas, and Kelly Vardiman. I especially wish to thank Pauline Colahan who edited the grammar and generally made the book easier to read.

CONTENTS

PREFACE

The Institute for Creation Research (ICR) has been sponsoring trips to the Grand Canyon since 1980. Through 1998 more than 2,000 people have joined us on these tours and most have indicated how enjoyable and significant these trips have been to their understanding of creation and the Genesis flood. The close fellowship and bonds that have developed between people from all over the United States and the world on these tours has been a joy to observe and in which to participate.

As you would expect, when large numbers of people get together for any kind of event, incidents are bound to occur which are sometimes funny at the time, but can be hilarious when recounted later. This is even more true when they occur in an environment which is sometimes unforgiving, like that of the Grand Canyon.

This book is an attempt to recall some of the funny and even embarrassing incidents which have occurred over some 15 years during my participation in Grand Canyon tours. Several happened on the backpacking trips, a few on the buses, and others on the rafts or where the groups stayed. A surprising number involved David McQueen, a good friend and a former professor at ICR. Although the book is focused on many of the humorous events of the Grand Canyon tours, I will also include experiences and impressions for those who would like to vicariously experience a trip to the canyon. I will also relate some of the geology and other technical discussions which are included in the lectures on our tours.

Except for ICR staff, guest leaders, and a few other guests who have given permission to use their names, all other persons mentioned in the book are fictitious to protect the innocent. All events actually occurred, although some license may have been used in describing where and on which trip several of them happened.

TWO DEAD BOY SCOUTS

THE DAY STARTED OUT pretty well. Sixteen backpackers had been dropped off at the Hermit Creek trail head near the west end of the Grand Canyon on Monday morning, ready to descend over the edge some 13 miles to the first night's camp. Dave McQueen and I were the leaders for this year's Hermit Creek hiking group. My specialty is atmospheric science, so I typically talk about the Ice Age, clouds, ice crystals, sunlight, weather, and climate, today and before the Genesis flood. I was the principal leader, so I gave most of the devotionals and general directions.

Dave McQueen is a geologist and a devoted rock collector. Dave takes his rocks so seriously that he carries all kinds of equipment to test rocks when he backpacks in the Grand Canyon. He wears a bright, red vest with multicolored patches indicating where he has traveled, pockets for maps, other pockets to hold pencils and pens, and things like a magnifying glass and bottles of acid dangling from loops. Dave lectured on geology and implications of the flood.

We had both led groups into the Grand Canyon several times before, but neither of us had ever been down this particular trail. We had studied the topographic and trail maps thoroughly, and because we were both experienced backpackers, we didn't have any great concern about reaching camp by nightfall.

However, because we didn't yet know the capabilities of this particular hiking group, we wanted to get started as soon as possible to be sure we reached our campsite at a reasonable hour. We had several lecture stops to make along the way. We needed to stop about 30 minutes down the trail to show the group an outstanding example of amphibian tracks in the Coconino sandstone. These tracks just off the trail would also allow us to make final adjustments to packs and offer suggestions on how to avoid foot blisters and sore shoulders from the packs.

The only hint that we might have a problem with this group was when Dan Oglesby insisted that he be allowed to carry a 50-pound pack, no matter how much we tried to convince him that he would enjoy the week much more with a lighter pack. Dan was a short, stocky salmon fisherman from Anchorage, Alaska, who insisted that he was used to carrying heavy loads and roughing it in the outback. Unfortunately, we found out later that he had never backpacked before and all of his food was canned. Based on our experience with Dan, all future backpackers are now required to complete a full pack inspection and limit their weight to no more than 40 pounds for men and 30 pounds for women.

Before starting down the trail, Dave McQueen led the group in calisthenics and I gave a short devotional on Moses in the wilderness. Many devotionals in the Grand Canyon focus on rocks, trees, and dry places. It seems appropriate to use objects near at hand to illustrate spiritual truth when camping. It's no wonder Christ used so many object lessons when He traveled around Israel. As we exercised and had devotions we became somewhat more familiar with the group of ten men and four women.

Two of the middle-aged men had brought their wives, and the two remaining women were single and in their thirties. Fran, one of the single women, was a medical doctor, although she preferred that the group not know that. It is difficult for medical people on backpacking trips, because if it is known that they are doctors or nurses, the group will sometimes expect medical advice on problems of all sorts, including minor accidents, during the trip. Medical liability also comes into play if they assist. If they prefer to remain anonymous, we don't inform the group about the presence of medical personnel on backpacking trips unless a medical emergency occurs.

Two of the young, single men in the group, Bob and Jim, were cross-country runners. They were in outstanding condition. Both were thin, wiry, and full of energy. In fact, as we descended the trail later in the day, they asked permission to go on ahead of the group to a fork in the trail where they would wait for us. However, when we were somewhat late in arriving, they dropped their packs and ran back up the trail to meet us, and then ran back down the trail again. I figure they added at least 10 miles to the full distance of 13 miles just jogging back and forth. Oh, for the strength of my youth!

By about ten o'clock we were able to start down the trail. This was two hours later than we had hoped. The bus had been late dropping us off because of a delay caused by other hiking groups getting to the Bright Angel and Grandview Trails on the east end of the Grand Canyon. Calisthenics, the devotional, and picture taking had delayed us another hour. But, finally we were on our way.

We hadn't gone more than a hundred yards when one of the group lost his bedroll and Lisa was having pain in her shoe. We stopped to refasten the bedroll and took a look at Lisa's foot. It turned out that the foot pain was from a new pair of shoes which hadn't been broken in. Although we discourage anyone from wearing new shoes on our trips, there is always someone who doesn't get the word. We decided to cut some moleskin for Lisa's foot to avoid blisters.

Moleskin is a wonderfully soft material that can be purchased at most sporting goods stores. It has soft, cotton material on one side and an adhesive on the other. It can be cut with scissors and fit to toes, heels, and other places on one's feet to prevent or alleviate blisters or other sore spots. Moleskin has been the theme of many songs written on our hiking trips to the Grand Canyon and often becomes a highly sought-after commodity near the end of a week of hiking. Moleskin and toilet paper are sometimes called "mountain money."

It took about 15 minutes to cut the patches and fit them to Lisa's feet before we were off again. As we traveled downward, we passed through layers of Kaibab limestone, the Toroweap formation, and into the top layers of the Coconino sandstone. All hikers are expected to learn the names of the layers by heart as they descend. In some years we have sold T-shirts with the rock layers printed on the front so that hikers can review the names as they face each other.

Each layer of rock has its own significance. The Kaibab limestone is filled with fossils of marine organisms, particularly brachiopods. These are bi-valved shell creatures which were common in oceans of the past. It is fascinating that marine organisms are abundant over miles of desert where there is little water today. Both the fossils and the limestone which make up the rock apparently precipitated from an ancient sea. However, the instruction from our leaders offers a young-earth, catastrophic explanation for the formation of these layers rather than the

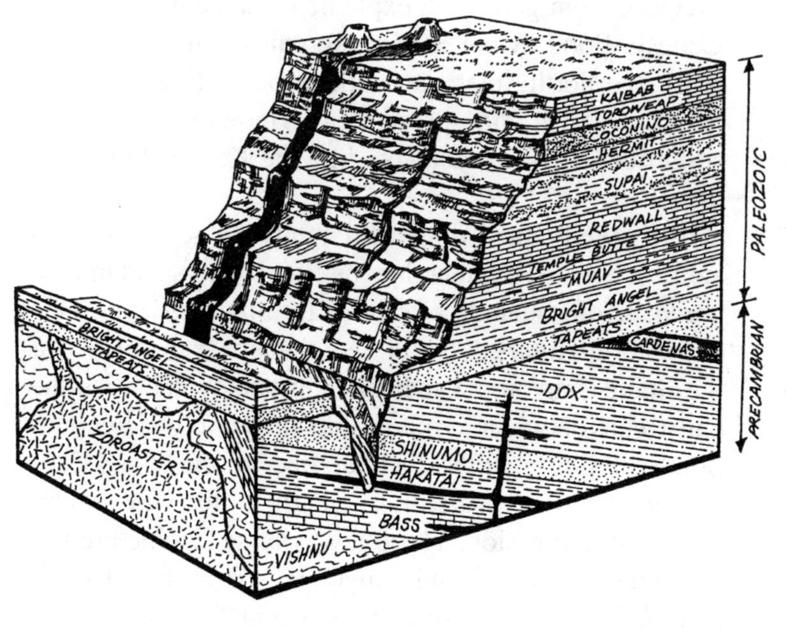

ROCK TYPES

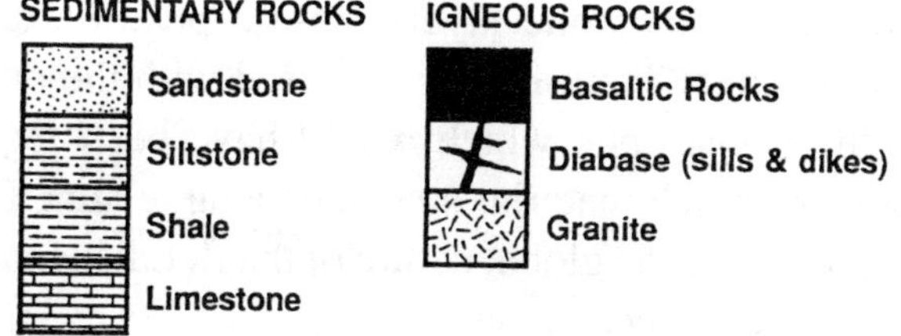

METAMORPHIC ROCKS

The vertical cross-section of Grand Canyon showing the various rock formations.

conventional millions-of-years explanation. Dave McQueen, our geologist, explained that the waters of the Genesis flood swept marine organisms and sea water across the North American continent depositing sediments and fossils over widespread areas. These sediments later solidified and formed layers like the Kaibab limestone layer.

As we walked down through the Coconino sandstone, it became evident that the flood waters had moved a tremendous quantity of sand in forming this layer. This white formation is 300–400 feet thick near the center of the Grand Canyon. It can be seen just below the lip of the entire canyon when looking from almost any viewpoint. Some call this layer the "bathtub ring" of the Grand Canyon because it can be seen so clearly all the way around this great depression. These layers of sandstone are not only present at the Grand Canyon in Arizona but also extend into California, New Mexico, and Texas as well as into Utah and Nevada. Such extensive, homogeneous layers would argue for massive deposition of sand in a single, large-scale event like the Genesis flood. In fact, when I first hiked the Grand Canyon and looked up at the Coconino sandstone layers from a position along the Bright Angel Trail, I was impressed with the magnitude of the catastrophe which would have been required to move so much material over such a large area. I became convinced of the global nature of the flood due to this one piece of evidence alone.

Embedded in the walls of the Coconino sandstone are not only horizontal lines separating the various strata as sand was laid down to form the rock but also inclined, cross-bedded lines. The conventional long-age geological explanation for this "cross-bedding" is that layers of sand were formed in dunes by wind in an ancient desert. The steepness would seem to be better explained by dune formation under moving water. In other words, these dunes seem to have been formed under hundreds of feet of water moving across a sea floor. The image of water hundreds of feet deep, hundreds of miles in lateral extent, moving at speeds of up to tens of miles per hour boggles the mind, but the evidence supports it.

Part way through the Coconino sandstone layer we stopped to look at footprints left in the sandstone by ancient amphibians. About 20 feet off the trail we located a large inclined rock layer with animal tracks embedded in it. There were several sets of tracks, but the most impressive trail was about ten feet long. The tracks were about six inches apart with an occasional line between them suggesting that the animal was a type of amphibian dragging its tail. In many locations these trails show the animal climbing the sand dune at an angle to the flow of the current across the dune. The animal apparently swam from the top of one dune to another because of missing tracks on portions of the dune.

The fact that the footprints remained in the rock is somewhat of a mystery. It would appear that the tracks must have been immediately covered by fresh deposits of sand which came in pulses. When the rock was exposed later, the layers eroded preferentially at the interface between pulses, exposing the tracks. This explanation would seem to imply that there may be many trackways still imbedded in the rock which have not yet been exposed.

Another fascinating mystery is why there were living animals leaving footprints so late in the flood. The Coconino sandstone is about 4,000 feet above the lowest sedimentary layer in the Grand Canyon. If almost a mile of sediment had already been laid down by the flood, how could some animals still be alive? Dinosaur tracks which are often found in the Morrison formation are located at even higher levels in the geologic strata. It would appear that some animals were able to escape the waters until later in the flood. Many were strong swimmers but they may have migrated to higher ground or clung to floating vegetation and were only killed later as the waters finally reached them. Dr. John Baumgardner, a research scientist at Los Alamos National Laboratory, has suggested that circulating water inundating the continents may have formed giant whirlpools with dry floors near the center until late in the flood. This may have allowed animals near the center of continents to initially escape the flood waters but were then overwhelmed when the events of the flood reached their zenith.

It had taken our hikers about an hour to reach the tracks in the Coconino sandstone, and by the time we had lectured on the formation of the rock strata and the features of the reptile tracks, it was almost noon. We decided to break out our lunches and eat before continuing on down the trail. I noticed that Dan was not eating his lunch, so I inquired if he was hungry. He said that he didn't feel like eating and would wait until a little later to have his lunch. He was adjusting the straps on his backpack, so I didn't think more about our conversation.

I encouraged everyone to drink plenty of water. It's easy in a dry climate like Arizona to forget to drink enough water. The body tends to lose a lot of water by perspiration even though it isn't evident by moisture on the skin. Some had brought powdered Gatorade to mix with the water in their canteens and I encouraged its use. Along with the loss of water, the body also eliminates minerals like sodium, potassium, and magnesium, which can lead to heat stroke. After a short lunch we started down the trail again. By this time the temperature was approaching 100°F and most of the group had put on sun screen to avoid sunburn.

The next part of the trail had been eroded badly with many small round pebbles lying on top of rock. The footing was very difficult with several of the group sliding and falling from time to time. After about five miles of this unstable footing, some of the group were beginning to tire. In particular, Dan was at the tail end of the group and having difficulty keeping up. I usually stay near the back of the group to help the stragglers and encourage them to keep moving. Dave McQueen had been hiking near the center of the group because he tends to stop often to explore various rock outcrops and lecture the group on geological features.

Bob and Jim, our two cross-country hikers, were becoming frustrated with the slow pace of the group, so I gave them permission to continue on alone down to the junction in the trail where it forked to the right toward our campground for the night. The fork was about ten miles from the trail head we had left earlier in the morning. By the time we were within about three miles of the junction, Bob and Jim had run back uphill to the group and were prancing in place while we slowly plodded downward. They ran back and forth several times between the junction and the group in the time it took us to reach the fork in the trail. They told me later that they normally run about 25 miles each day, just to stay in shape.

The afternoon heat was beginning to tell on Dan. He was going extremely slowly and was having to stop from time to time for rest. By the time the group reached the junction, it was supper time, so we decided to stop and eat. We still had three miles to go to reach camp for the night and it was becoming evident that we had a problem. Dave McQueen offered to stay with Dan and walk slowly with him and I agreed to lead the main group into camp. Night fell about a mile from the junction and we had to break out flashlights in order to see our way in the dark. I had never hiked the canyon in the dark, particularly on an unfamiliar trail, but fortunately the trail was well marked and we made it to camp without any incidents.

However, when we got to camp, we had difficulty finding the group camp site. We were so tired from the long day and 13-mile hike that after 15 minutes hunting for it unsuccessfully, I finally gave permission to set up camp near the base of a cliff that looked like it might be the correct spot.

After we settled into camp and rested for a while, Bob and Jim came over to my tent and asked if I had seen Dave McQueen and Dan. I said that they hadn't shown up yet. They offered to go back up the trail and look for them if I wished. I told them to wait another half-hour and if Dave and Dan hadn't shown up by then, they could go check on them. By about 9:30 p.m. they still hadn't appeared, so Bob and Jim went to look for them. They came back an hour later and reported that Dan had become ill and couldn't continue on. Dave had decided to camp on the trail for the night and come into camp in the morning. Since there was little any of us could do for them, I decided to proceed with the regular group activities and wait for them to arrive the next day.

Unfortunately, in the morning light next day it became evident that the camp site we had selected was about 1/8 mile from where the group camp site was actually located, so we had to move our tents. Since we were going to stay at this site for two more nights, rather than taking down the tents, we just pulled up stakes and carried the tents on our heads. That must have been quite a sight, watching a line of about a dozen multicolored tents moving in single file along the trail from one camp site to another! It probably looked something like a centipede bumping along the trail.

By about 9:00 a.m. Dave and Dan arrived in camp. We helped Dan get his tent set up and he immediately crawled into it and stayed there for the next four days. He had apparently caught the flu on his way to the Grand Canyon from Alaska and was fully involved by the time he was part way down the trail. We kept him hydrated by carrying water bottles to his tent, but he didn't eat until the last night we were in camp. Fortunately, we had some expert medical help in Fran, who assisted him in the situation or we might have had to call for a helicopter rescue.

Not long after Dave and Dan rejoined the group, a park ranger walked into the campground and asked for the group leader. When he was directed to me, he asked if we had any boy scouts in our group. I told him no and asked why he wanted to know. He said that a camper had just hiked from this campground to the next camping area beyond the junction and had passed two people camped on the trail. The hiker had reported to the ranger station near the second camping area that there appeared to be two dead boy scouts on the trail! However, in hiking over the same path to reach our camp, the two were no longer there and he was trying to locate them.

After a few moments of confusion, I realized he was talking about Dave McQueen and Dan Oglesby. The two dead boy scouts were Dave and Dan! The hikers had seen Dave's red vest with all the multicolored patches and attached geologic equipment on it while he slept on the trail and mistook him for a boy scout. They were sleeping so soundly that they appeared to be dead.

When I explained to the ranger who the "dead boy scouts" were, he didn't find it amusing but wanted to write us a citation for camping in an unapproved area. After explaining how Dan had become ill and we had decided to allow him to remain on the trail overnight until he improved somewhat, the ranger reluctantly agreed not to cite us. However, he sternly warned me not to allow anyone to camp on the trail again or I would face a stiff fine.

I learned later from Dave McQueen that there was a lot more to this story than at first met the eye. Apparently, the park ranger who had almost given us a citation had been having problems with the group of hikers who reported Dave and Dan as dead boy scouts on the trail. The ranger had found them swimming naked in the Colorado River the previous day, revoked their camping permits, and fined them $100 each. They were on their way out of the canyon in a foul mood when they passed Dave and Dan asleep on the trail. Because they were angry at the ranger, they decided to report Dave and Dan to the ranger in order to force him to make the prolonged walk several miles down the trail to our campsite. When the ranger arrived at our campsite he had already been through several confrontations. Fortunately, after several minutes of discussion and explanations, he became reasonable and treated us professionally.

The remainder of the trip was enjoyable for all except Dan Oglesby, who remained in his tent all week. He finally improved on Friday evening, the night before we were to hike out again. By that time he had grown hungry and was ready to eat a hearty meal. However, even a salmon fisherman could not eat the 20 pounds of canned goods he had brought in his backpack. In order to lighten his pack for the trip to the top, we passed around his cans of stew, smoked salmon, and baked beans to share among the group. Dan made it out of the canyon and is today remembered as one of the two dead boy scouts!

Two dead boy scouts on the trail.

FROM UP HERE YOU CAN BE SEEN FOREVER

ONE OF MY FAVORITE viewpoints in the Grand Canyon is the top of Horseshoe Mesa east of Grand Canyon Village. Horseshoe Mesa is located about three miles down Grandview Trail and is a horseshoe-shaped outcrop of limestone above the Tonto Platform. The two prongs of the horseshoe extend northward toward the Colorado River with the cleat near the back of the horseshoe composed of layers of the Supai group facing upward at the south wall of the canyon.

Horseshoe Mesa now sits on top of the redwall limestone with the overlying layers eroded away. It appears red in most places because the natural gray limestone has been stained by the solution of iron oxide dissolved in rainwater from the soft, red Supai group above coating the limestone beneath. In a few places where the Supai group above is missing, the limestone retains its natural gray color.

At the edge of Horseshoe Mesa is a nearly 400-foot vertical cliff. Magnificent views of the canyon can be seen at the brink of this cliff. One can stand and look down to the Colorado River beyond the Tonto Platform below. When two backpacking groups are simultaneously scheduled for Cottonwood Creek and Hance Creek, below and to opposite sides of Horseshoe Mesa, the two groups typically meet for lunch on one of the days and combine staff to talk about the geology of the Inner Gorge. They meet

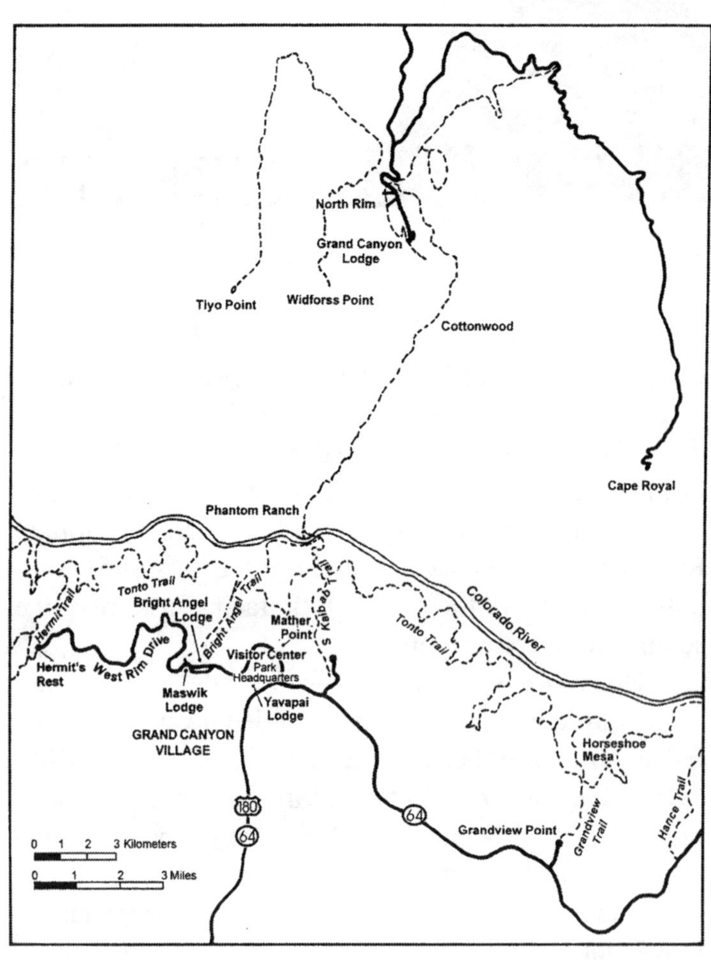

A map of the hiking trails near Horseshoe Mesa.

at the edge of the Tonto Platform to the northeast and below Horseshoe Mesa on a promontory which overlooks the inner gorge. The site lies directly over the river so that it is possible to spit into the water over 1,000 feet below. Looking down from Horseshoe Mesa, one can see the trail descending along the edge of the cliff and out along the Tonto Platform. Various other trails appear white against the bluish-green vegetation as they branch and intersect when crossing Hance Creek and travel along the edge of the Tonto Platform.

Upstream to the east of Horseshoe Mesa one can see the river working its way downward through the various layers until it reaches the black, crystalline rock below the sedimentary layers. The Inner Gorge is as much as 1,500 feet deep in places and is composed of Vishnu schist and Zoroaster granite. The horizontal sedimentary layer just above the crystalline rock in central Grand Canyon is called the Tapeats sandstone. The boundary between these two rock layers is called the Great Unconformity because not only does the color, composition, and orientation of the rocks change suddenly over a vertical distance of only a millimeter or so, but the rocks also change from sedimentary to igneous or metamorphic.

In eastern Grand Canyon the situation is slightly more complex because a dipping layer of strata known as the Grand Canyon Supergroup occurs above the Great Unconformity between the crystalline rock and the Tapeats sandstone. The Great Unconformity exists for hundreds of miles in every direction from the Grand Canyon and is recognized as a level at which a major change in earth processes occurred.

Sedimentary rock is formed by the hardening of sand or mud which has been deposited by water. Igneous rock is formed by the cooling of hot, liquid rock. At the Great Unconformity there is evidence that a catastrophic movement of water and sediment swept across the surface of the Vishnu schist and Zoroaster granite, which had been formed earlier from magma, planing off this underlying layer and then depositing the first sedimentary layer. At this boundary, which is a favorite spot for our tour participants to visit, there are many boulders, some as large as a dump truck, embedded in the Tapeats sandstone just above the interface. These boulders are composed of Shinumo quartzite, derived from the Grand Canyon Supergroup. Some are rounded like river rock, but others still have jagged edges, as if they were not carried far before they were redeposited. Surrounding many of the boulders are flow patterns in the sediment showing how the sand was deposited in a fast-moving stream of water.

The velocity of water required to rip up and move boulders the size of cars and trucks would probably approach tens of miles per hour. At these speeds, water containing sediment can move large objects and tear apart solid rock. A release of flood waters through the flood-control tunnels at Glen Canyon Dam in 1983 eroded large pits in solid concrete and rock in only minutes. The U.S. Bureau of Reclamation found that high-velocity flows of water cause cavitation to occur which can be very destructive. Cavitation is the explosive action of small bubbles on rock or steel when they are formed in water moving at high velocities near a sharp obstruction. These small bubbles produce jackhammer like shocks on rock when they form and then collapse.

Such a massive flood of water and sediments has been proposed as an explanation for some of the surface features on Mars. Yet today there is practically no water on Mars. On earth, where about 70 percent of its surface is covered with water several miles deep, such a flood is ridiculed. Yet, at the bottom of the Grand Canyon is evidence that an even greater flood may have occurred on earth. This flood eroded large areas of the earth and then redeposited a layer of new sediment several miles deep.

This evidence strongly supports the worldwide cataclysm described in Genesis.

Not only is Horseshoe Mesa and vicinity a good place to see large-scale geological features, but it is also a beautiful place to observe scenery. I suspect the top of Horseshoe Mesa was a favorite spot for the Anasazi, because backpackers on several tours have found at least one chipping station where arrowheads were made on top of the mesa. If you were an Native American and you needed to spend days making arrowheads by pressing an antelope horn against the edge of a flint rock, you would probably also wish to find a place with a view while you worked.

Near the eastern edge of Horseshoe Mesa, the view is magnificent, particularly in the evening. As you stand near the edge, you can see the valley below shrouded in shadows as the sun sets behind you to the west. The rosy remains of the sun slowly climb up the walls before you. A light wind typically rises near the edge of the cliff at your feet providing an updraft for eagles to soar on one last flight of the day.

For three years in a row I was privileged to be standing in this location not far from camp in the evening, when a golden eagle, without knowing I was there, flew along the edge of the cliff toward me until he was about 20 feet away. Each year when he saw me, he screeched that beautiful cry of the eagle and barrel-rolled away from me down into the valley below and flew to his perch a mile away. At that moment I felt the call of the wild and understood the pleasure Native Americans have in wide-open spaces.

On days when the wind is blowing strongly, Horseshoe Mesa takes on an entirely different character. Wind gusts can sweep across the top of the mesa at 50 miles per hour, ripping up tents and driving dust and sand deep into the pores of your skin. After several hours of wind on top of the mesa, you will have red sand in your eyes, ears, and nose. Trying to sleep at night on the mesa when the wind is blowing can be difficult. Even if you have your tent staked down well, it tends to flatten in the wind and dance at every gust. It is interesting to listen for the next gust to blow down the canyon. You can often hear it whistling first in the rocks and trees several hundred yards away and getting louder as it comes closer. When it hits your tent, you just hope you won't be carried over the edge of the cliff.

If it rains while you are in the canyon, you may be blessed with a light, gentle rain. But in summer, you are more likely to experience thunderstorms which can dump an inch of rain in 15 minutes or so. Thunderstorms can turn the canyon's streams into muddy torrents from every gully and cliff. Rain does not soak into the ground but runs off all of the rocky surfaces almost as soon as it falls. Small gullies can become streams; small streams, rivers; and rivers, a torrent. It is awe-inspiring to watch water falling in sheets and waves from cliffs surrounding you. The noise of large raindrops hitting the ground, water splashing from cliffs above, and thunder echoing among the side canyons can be intimidating.

But when the rain stops, and the water quits flowing a few minutes later, you will think you are in heaven. If it's late in the afternoon, brilliant rainbows break out toward the east. The fresh smell of soil and sage after a rain permeates the air and the sound of the canyon wren and other birds signal a fresh start. This must have been something like what Noah experienced after the flood.

The views and experiences on Horseshoe Mesa are some of my favorite memories. However, the view which inspired the title of this chapter is yet to be described. In the early 1980s the National Park Service decided to install pit toilets at several locations throughout the park because of the increasing numbers of backpackers. One of the selected sites was atop Horseshoe Mesa. Two group campsites and an area for individual campers were located on the southeastern end of the mesa near where the Cottonwood and Hance Creek Trails split and drop over the edge of the mesa to the valleys below.

Because all the materials for the toilet had to be either airlifted or brought in by pack mule, the construction was done over a two-year period. Our group first visited Horseshoe Mesa after the first half of the construction had been completed. When we arrived on Horseshoe Mesa, the first hikers to search for the toilet were Gwen and Connie, who were unaccustomed to the crudeness of outdoor life. They had already complained about the lack of facilities on the trail down and were eager to avail themselves of the modern pit toilets advertised on our trail guides.

They followed a sign which pointed north and said "Toilet 1/8 mile." While they were gone, the rest of us began to put up our tents and cook supper. Gwen and Connie were gone about 20 minutes and when they came back, they marched directly up to Steve and me and demanded to know if we were trying to be funny. If we were, they didn't think it was funny, and they had a good mind to hike right back up the trail and go home!

"What are you talking about?" Steve said. "We aren't trying to be funny."

Gwen became even more adamant and said, "That toilet you sent us to isn't a toilet. It's a travesty. If you think we are going to use that, you've got another think coming. Go look at it! You'll see what I mean."

Of course, the whole group had overheard this exchange and couldn't help but wonder what was going on. So when Steve and I headed toward the toilet to find out what the problem was, the whole group decided to tag along.

It took about five minutes to walk to the facility. The park service had nicely placed little rocks along both sides of the trail, so it would be easy to follow in the dark. By

The half-completed outhouse on Horseshoe Mesa.

the time we neared the toilet, it was twilight and a quarter moon was just coming up over the eastern end of the canyon. We climbed a small hill, circled around a large boulder, and walked past a small tree before coming out onto a clearing where the toilet was supposed to be.

However, instead of finding the expected rustic, wooden outhouse, perched before us was a white, metal bowl built on a wooden platform ten feet square and about a foot above the ground. There were no walls and a single post was positioned in front with a roll of paper hanging from it. Beyond the toilet was the most magnificent 360-degree view of the canyon anyone could ever want The moon was rising majestically off to one side.

The entire group came to a sudden stop, paused for about 5 seconds, and immediately burst into fits of laughter. Gwen and Connie, who had tagged along at the rear of the group, immediately turned and walked back to camp without a single word.

Later that evening during devotions, the group apologized to Gwen and Connie for laughing and promised to help set guards near the toilet to keep prying eyes away whenever they needed to use it. In fact, we established the rule that two people at a time had to visit the toilet in order to establish a watch.

The next year when we returned to Horseshoe Mesa, the toilet no longer had a 360-degree view. The park service had completed its construction. Some of the more remote campsites like Salt and Horn Creek between Indian Gardens and Monument still have outhouses with no walls except for a few bushes. Although I prefer privacy when I'm in a toilet, I sometimes miss the view we had that year atop Horseshoe Mesa. That pit toilet probably had the most incredible scenery a contemplative person could ever desire for his daily ministrations.

HEY, I HAVE ONE OF THOSE!

WHEN YOU HIKE THE Grand Canyon, there is often a temptation to pick up rocks and fossils to bring home as souvenirs. However, it is against the law to remove any object from a national park without special permission. This includes rocks, fossils, arrowheads, plants, etc. When you look at the dry, desolate mountains, valleys, and mesas, most people can't imagine what harm there could be to pick up a rock now and then to take home. However, when you consider that the number of visitors to the Grand Canyon each year is approaching five million, you can imagine the damage that would be done to the trails and sites if each person simply took one rock or fossil.

In years past, the rules were not so stringent and backpackers commonly carried rock hammers to chip off a rock sample for their collection. If you are seen carrying a rock hammer on your belt today, a ranger will stop you and probably ask to check your pack. If he finds any rocks or other objects from the canyon, you could face a stiff fine. Our backpackers and rafters are informed of these rules and warned not to collect any samples.

The park service will allow research organizations to collect samples if a request is made ahead of time and the project is found to be a worthy effort. Dave McQueen made the first application to Grand Canyon National Park for permission to collect rock samples. Dr. Austin and other associates have made additional applications in the years following. These requests have normally been granted and some of our guests have been willing to help lug heavy rocks from the bottom of the canyon.

Samples have been collected from a large number of the formations in the Grand Canyon, particularly layers containing igneous rock. These samples are prepared for analysis in several radioisotope laboratories to estimate the time since their formation. The preparation of the samples involves crushing the rock into powder. They are then sent for potassium-argon and rubidium-strontium analyses in commercial and academic laboratories where the elements are separated from the crushed rock. Analyses in these laboratories are routinely done on samples collected by researchers from all over the world and findings compared with accepted standards. The typical cost for a single sample is about $400.

The results have been very interesting. Samples of lava from volcanoes which have erupted within historic time on the north rim of the canyon west of Grand Canyon Village have given dates of millions of years since their formation from the magma. This is not reasonable, because these eruptions were reported by the Indians and organic material buried in the lava has been dated by carbon-14 methods as occurring within the last few thousand years. In addition, layers of igneous rock embedded in and between the sedimentary layers of the canyon give dates which are younger than the lava which flowed over them. The various methods of dating the rock also give widely discordant dates. These results have been published in several reports and journals.

The conclusion from these efforts is that the techniques which are used to date rocks are highly suspect. The lack of consistency between dating methods and the illogical sequences of events lead one to discount any dates derived. The assumption that rock layers in the Grand Canyon were formed millions of years ago by slow, steady processes does not hold up under rigorous investigation.

Dr. Austin and Dr. Andrew Snelling, two creationist geologists, are continuing to collect rock samples from the Grand Canyon for further analyses. They hope to be able to discredit the current dating methods and to develop an alternative understanding of the Grand Canyon strata within a young-earth time frame. Donations for laboratory analyses are always welcome.

The best means of collecting rocks for the past few years has been by raft. When rafting trips are scheduled, the overnight stops are partially selected to allow rock collection from the outcrops along the river. One other major benefit of collecting rocks on a raft trip is that the rocks can be floated downstream on the rafts and transported back home without having to carry them out in backpacks. At the end of the raft trip the rafters, rafts, supplies, and rock samples are transported to the rim of the canyon by bus. Of course, strong backs are still needed to climb from the river up to the outcrops, break off the samples, and carry them down to the rafts. (If you decide to join our raft trip, let us know if you wish to help collect rock samples.)

In the early years of our trips to the Grand Canyon, several of our scientists carried rock hammers on their belts to help collect rock samples. We no longer do this, even when we have permits to collect samples, because of the public relations image we wish to maintain. It is not commonly known that collection permits are granted for research projects. If rangers or visitors to the canyon see our group carrying rock hammers, they often assume we are typical "amateurs" who are out to destroy the canyon. When we need special tools for rock collection, they are carried out of sight in our packs.

A rock collecting tool was the source of a humorous incident one year on the Hance Creek trip. Dave McQueen had been asked to prepare a list of equipment for all backpack groups one year. He listed a full page of items which included the typical list of equipment such as food, socks, moleskin, tents, stoves, etc. He even drew a picture of a backpack and showed approximately where to store each item to make it easily accessible.

Dave warned the potential backpackers not to pack too many items or carry too heavy a pack. He indicated that this would contribute to blisters and lead to more work carrying the pack than was necessary. However, he couldn't resist adding several items which he believed no one would take seriously and bring with them. For example, he suggested that if anyone wished to help collect rock samples, they should bring a large crowbar.

When the Hance Creek group assembled for final instructions on Sunday afternoon before starting down into the canyon, they were shown how to use the water filters to purify the drinking water and how to prevent blisters on their feet. They were advised to carry four quarts of water and use Gatorade or Gookinade during hot weather. And finally, they were strongly advised to share as much equipment with a partner as possible to reduce the weight of their packs for the week. The nine men and five women listened intently and made the suggested adjustments. Although a few in the group were a little uncertain about what to expect, most seemed confident and ready to go.

Following are selected items from Dave McQueen's equipment list.

SCIENTIFIC EXPEDITION CHECKLIST
ICR GRAND CANYON HIKING GROUPS — 1986
by David R. McQueen, M.S., Asst. Prof. of Geology

Important Note: YOU ARE NOT EXPECTED TO BRING ALL THE ITEMS ON THIS LIST. Professor McQueen will have 95 percent of these items on his person, so if, for example, you want to see a geologic compass demonstrated, it will be available on the rim and in the bus. The fact that there is a compass on the list does not mean you must bring it. Use common sense.

1. Bible, stored in your heart and pack
2. Boots or shoes, tennis (court vs track)
3. Dark glasses
4. Five "1 quart" water bottles, with one on a belt hanger
5. The "salt" replacement additive called ERG (Gookinade), one per day
23. Tent, check for stakes and poles
26. 35 mm camera, with 50 mm lens
33. Drinking cup, collapsing
34. Pocket knife
77. Coffee, with sugar and cream premixed
79. Powdered eggs
88. Hard chocolate
162. Hammer, pick
163. Hammer, sledge, 10 lb. (note, teenagers are limited to the 2 lb. sledge
179. Nuclear weapons, tactical, "Kiloton range"
220. Water balloons, 77/person/day of desert warfare

The group descended the Grandview Trail to

HEY, I HAVE ONE OF THOSE!

Horseshoe Mesa without incident and then continued on down the steep trail off the redwall limestone to the Hance Creek campsite in the valley below. On this portion of the trail two members of the group found out that they had a mild fear of heights. The trail coming off the mesa is only two or three feet wide in places and is steep and rocky. In addition, the trail is cut into the redwall limestone so that an overhang forces the backpackers to squat as their backpacks pass under the rock above. The cliff to the side of this overhang drops vertically for about 200 feet. I always had difficulty with this section of the trail because I carry a large bedroll fastened to the top of my pack. It is a piece of four-inch rolled-up foam. Because it extends a foot or more above my head and makes me look as if I'm carrying an extremely heavy load, I was given the name "The Missouri Mule" by Dave McQueen. If one is not careful, such an ungainly backpack will hit the wall or roof and unexpectedly thrust a careless hiker toward the waiting void.

Anyone coming to this portion of the trail will have second thoughts about continuing, and when the wind blows dust from the trail into your eyes and buffets you around, some have considered giving up in sheer, stark terror. Every year or so the park service reports that backpackers have fallen from this location and been killed on the rocks below because they were not as careful as they should have been.

Fortunately, no one on any trips I've been on has ever had a serious accident here or anywhere else in the canyon. We have had a few sprains and medical problems, but none of them have resulted in any permanent injury. Probably the most serious incident happened on a previous tour when one of our backpackers was blown off the Kaibab Trail on the way home during a strong wind. He was literally picked up and thrown down a slope off the trail. Fortunately, his fall was stopped by a large cactus which prevented him from going over a cliff. However, he was punctured by multiple cactus needles and needed minor surgery to remove some of them.

On the current tour, the group made it to the Hance Creek campsite without incident and spent a week there. During the week, they met the Cottonwood Creek group out on the Tonto Platform promontory overlooking the Inner Gorge, and conducted other day-hikes to such places as the Great Unconformity. They spent one night at the Colorado River where they met the raft group for supper and had breakfast with them the next morning. This is always a special treat for the Hance Creek hikers because they get to share in the great food served by the rafting companies. Typically, the evening meal offers large helpings of spaghetti with real french bread spread with butter and garlic seasoning. For backpackers, after eating Rice-A-Roni or chicken noodle soup all week, this is like Thanksgiving dinner!

The last night at the Hance Creek campsite turned chilly and windy. The wind was so strong that some decided to abandon their tents and sleep in cavities of the Tapeats sandstone near the campsite. During supper time it was a difficult chore keeping the stoves going to cook supper. Between supper and the evening devotions Dave McQueen began to investigate a large rock in the middle of camp which had fallen from the cliff above. It appeared to have some fossils in it, so it probably came from the redwall limestone or maybe even from the Kaibab limestone farther up.

As Dave explored the rock looking for fossils, many of the group gathered around helping him search. Among them, Frank Roberts seemed particularly impressed. When Dave came upon an especially nice specimen, he tried to pry it out of the rock with his fingers. After several minutes, he grew frustrated and exclaimed, "I sure wish I had my crowbar!" referring to his inclusion of the item in the equipment list. With only a moment's hesitation, Frank responded, "Hey, I've got one of those in my pack!" He then turned and walked over to his backpack and pulled out a two-foot long, three-pound crowbar and returned to the rock, offering it to Dave to use on the fossil.

For probably one of the few times in his life, Dave was speechless. I'm sure he never expected anyone to carry a crowbar into the canyon based on his bogus entry in the equipment list. Also knowing Dave as I do, I'm sure he would never have wanted to hurt anyone's feelings about such a misunderstanding. I'm confident he was struggling with how to respond to this gesture of good will.

Frank offers his crowbar to Dave McQueen to assist in extracting a fossil from a rock.

Dave finally said, "Thanks, Frank. This is just what I needed," as he proceeded to dig the fossil out of the rock and proclaim, "Now, this is as beautiful a specimen as I've ever seen. Here's your crowbar, Frank. Thanks, I'm done with it."

The crowbar incident has been one of those stories that has never until now received much open discussion. From time to time people will refer to the crowbar, but no one says much about Frank or whether he ever knew that it was not intended to be seriously considered as part of the suggested equipment list. However, the next year we revised the equipment list and wrote it in a more "straight-forward" manner so that no one would mistake what was actually intended to be brought on a backpacking trip.

COWPOKES ON THE TRAIL

BEFORE ONE ARRIVES at the Grand Canyon for the first time, he may have already constructed a mental image of what he expects to see. One of the strongest images typically comes from the song "On the Trail" from *Grand Canyon Suite,* in which the loping rhythm of the music imitates the cadence of the mules carrying visitors over the edge to Phantom Ranch at the river and back.

The experience of riding a mule nine miles to the Colorado River at first seems like a very romantic notion. What could be more exciting than riding tall in the saddle out West where the buffalo roam and the antelope play? In fact, when you first get on one of the mules at the Grand Canyon and start down the trail, you feel about ten feet tall and on top of the world. This is actually because the mules at Grand Canyon Village are some of the largest mules you'll see anywhere. When you are mounted, you are literally ten feet above the ground. When you first start down the trail, the canyon is spread out below you and the far side of the canyon is some 20 miles away.

Although the trail is at least six feet wide in most places to accommodate the large number of hikers sharing the trail with the mules, and even wider much of the time, it seems too narrow to contain your giant mule. Your eyes at first are glued to the mule's feet as he nonchalantly walks down the trail, apparently unconcerned that one misstep could send you and him to oblivion over the 500-foot cliff at your side. This trepidation is intensified whenever you pass a hiker coming up the trail. You are uncertain whether your mule will be frightened by the hiker and stumble or accidentally step off into space.

After about ten minutes you began to realize that these mules were selected for trail duty in the Grand Canyon because of their almost religious sense of duty in ignoring all the activity around them and plodding down the trail in single file behind the lead mule. The only remaining consternation is the occasional unexpected plunge downward when your mule steps over a log to a lower step in the trail. The first few times that happens, your heart is in your throat before you can reassure yourself that you aren't falling to your death.

Most groups who ride down the Bright Angel Trail go in groups of about 12 to 15. No one who weighs more than 200 pounds may ride a mule, so those who are overweight, like me, are consigned to walking. Most who take the mule ride down stay overnight at Phantom Ranch near the Colorado River on the north side. If you look carefully from several places on the rim, you can see the green cottonwood trees along Bright Angel Creek, where Phantom Ranch is located. The ranch has a bunkhouse, restaurant, snack shop, telephone, and post office. Reservations for a night in the bunkhouse need to be made several months ahead. You can write a postcard and have it stamped at Phantom Ranch. It is carried by leather pouch daily on the same mule train you ride into and out of the canyon.

The "wranglers" who lead the mule trains look like they've been doing this job for years. They typically wear faded jeans, leather chaps, boots, a black western shirt, and an old beat-up cowboy hat. I've never seen one of these wranglers with a new cowboy hat. I believe they are trying to avoid the "drugstore cowboy" look and go to the opposite extreme. Their hats, when they aren't wearing them, look like they've been stepped on by their mule and thrown into the back of their pickup truck. I suspect cowboys who ride mules may be making a statement with their hats. Maybe they are trying to distance themselves from the greenhorns in the mule train who sometimes wear pink cowboy hats or Indian headdresses.

Some of the wranglers are young men and women, but most are in their forties or older and look like they've been out in the weather most of their lives. Their skin is brown from the sun and as wrinkled as the mail pouches they carry. I'm always amazed at how thin cowboys are. Western shirts are cut with a long, narrow tail. Yet I've seen few working cowboys with a paunch. Apparently, pinto beans are not fattening.

The trail from Grand Canyon Village to Phantom Ranch takes about five hours by mule. The top part of the trail winds rapidly downward though the Kaibab limestone, the Toroweap formation, the Coconino sandstone, and into the hermit shale and the Supai group. The Kaibab limestone and Coconino sandstone are relatively hard rock, so they form vertical cliffs. The trail descends rapidly through these rock layers and is carved into the cliff face. In places the trail is cut through short tunnels. Frequently, along the trail you will see splashes of red color on the side, created by Indian Paintbrush clinging to cracks in the rock. The view is magnificent to the north, with hazy layers of multicolored rock off in the distance and reddish cliffs below you catching the morning sun.

Once the trail reaches the Supai group it flattens out somewhat and the going is not so steep. The Supai group is red oxidized sandstone and mudstone. It is much softer and does not generally form cliffs. There is also more vegetation along this part of the trail near the limited water supplies.

As you move down the trail, the heat increases dramatically. The temperature in the spring is typically about 40°F at seven o'clock in the morning when the mule train leaves the rim. It rises to about 100°F by noon at the river. Half of this change (30°F) is due to the heating by the sun during the day, but the other half is due to the increase in temperature as a function of altitude. Even on cloudy days and at night, the temperature at the river is typically 30°F warmer than it is at the rim 5,000 feet higher.

Because of the dramatic change in temperature and precipitation with elevation, the plant communities also change dramatically. Near the south rim at 7,000 feet elevation is a ponderosa pine forest which turns to pinion and juniper just below the rim. At about 5,000 feet the vegetation turns to blackbrush scrub and at about 3,000 feet to Mojave Desert scrub. Near the Colorado River the riparian woodland composed of cottonwood, redbud, and tamarisk dominates.

By the time you reach the Indian Gardens campground about 3-1/2 miles from the rim, you are ready for a restroom break and a drink of water. Fortunately, there is a water fountain at Indian Gardens and benches to sit on. However, when you get off your mule, you will soon find that you just want to walk or stand. Your backside is beginning to exhibit the early stages of soreness. Before you reach the river, you will be begging to get off your mule and walk. Unfortunately, once you start on a mule ride, you are required to stay on it the entire way. Although mules are selected for their surefootedness, they do not ride easily. They don't come with shock absorbers and they tend to be so wide that you will walk bowlegged for some time after you get off. The insides of your legs and knees tend to become raw from the constant chaffing against the stirrup straps and your back may become quite sore.

The Indian Gardens campground is one of the sites where our backpackers often stay during the Grand Canyon tour. Bright Angel Trail goes directly through the campsite and as many as 10,000 people per day may hike this trail during some busy weeks in the canyon. The campsite is located at the base of the redwall limestone and provides a spectacular view out of your tent in the morning when the sun rises. The light diffused from the cliffs causes the entire campsite to glow red in the morning and evening.

Cottonwood trees line the small stream that flows through the camp, providing a lush, green background to the area. Frequently, mule deer can be seen eating grass near the campground. Hawks, canyon wrens, hummingbirds, and an occasional golden eagle can be seen around the cliffs. Park rangers live in bunk houses at Indian Gardens and patrol the trails in all directions.

Bright Angel Trail was named after the Bright Angel shale on which the Indian Gardens campground sits. Bright Angel shale is easily fractured, and because of its soft nature and that of the muav just above it, a relatively flat bench called the Tonto Platform extends throughout most of the Grand Canyon . This platform permits easy hiking on trails parallel to the river. Beautiful fields of flowers grow on this platform and blossom in spring following plentiful rain. Some of the flowers found here are the beavertail cactus, prickly pear cactus, aster, Indian paintbrush, cushion flower, orange hollyhock, primrose, and verbena.

Bright Angel Trail continues down to the river and

up the north side of the canyon some 20 miles to the north rim. It follows the Bright Angel Fault which runs across the canyon from near Grand Canyon Village north-northeast to the north rim. Numerous faults run north and south, but there does not appear to be an east-west fault along the river.

The park service discourages hikers and runners from traveling the entire length of the Bright Angel Trail in one day; however, many do so. Some will even run the 20-mile length both ways in one day. I would strongly discourage anyone who is not in tiptop shape from attempting such a trip, especially during warmer weather of late spring through early fall. More and more people are experiencing heat stroke and other medical problems because they underestimate the rigor of hiking the canyon.

Although adults often don't use common sense when hiking the canyon, I am told that even small children can hike the canyon safely if they understand their limitations. One year when hiking the Kaibab Trail, which runs from Phantom Ranch to the rim east of the Bright Angel Trail, I noticed small tennis shoe impressions in the dust on the trail. They looked to be about size six and didn't seem to be accompanied by an adult, so I inquired of a ranger later in the trip about the wisdom of a child's traveling alone on such a trail. He replied, "Oh, you must have seen Amy's footprints."

Of course, I wanted to know who Amy was. He said, "Well, Amy is the seven-year-old daughter of one of the couples who runs the bunkhouse at Phantom Ranch. She goes to school in Grand Canyon Village and has to walk up to the rim each morning to catch the school bus. She walks back home each evening. It's only ten miles each way." When I was a child, I used to ride a bicycle three miles each way to school, but I didn't have to climb out of a canyon to do it. I assume the ranger wasn't pulling my leg, but, you never know. You hear a lot of tall tales in the West.

After a short break at the Indian Gardens Campground, the mule train is ready to continue on down the trail to the river. There is a choice of several trails out of Indian Gardens. The Tonto Trail runs east and west at this point and other campsites are available along this trail. A short trail also extends directly northward to Plateau Point overlooking the Inner Gorge, similar to the one near Horseshoe Mesa. However, the view here is not as dramatic. Near this overlook, what appear to be fossil footprints of four-footed vertebrates have been discovered in the Tapeats sandstone. Walter Barnhart, a former ICR graduate student who wrote his thesis refuting the evolution of the horse, has mapped these tracks and believes some of the them may have been made by a lion. The Tapeats sandstone here is the first layer above the Great Unconformity and would, therefore, indicate that these prints were formed early in the flood. According to evolutionary theory, only marine invertebrates should be found this low in the sedimentary strata. They call these vertebrate footprints "anomalous fossils" because they are in the wrong place if evolution is true.

Shortly below Indian Gardens the Bright Angel Trail begins to descend quickly again down through the Tapeats sandstone, the last sedimentary layer above the crystalline basement rock of Vishnu schist and Zoroaster granite. The trail follows a creek which first became noticeable at Indian Gardens. Dense brush, trees, and blackberry bushes fill the creek bed. About two miles farther along the trail we finally reach the Great Unconformity and leave the Tapeats sandstone. The Vishnu schist and Zoroaster granite are very hard and produce steep cliffs in places. Consequently, the trail has many switchbacks and produces dramatic overlooks. The view from muleback once again induces fear in the riders, but our faithful mode of transportation seems as sure-footed as ever.

Hiking somewhere along the lower part of this trail I observed one of the most amazing sights I've ever seen as a backpack leader. Steve Austin and I were leading a group of backpackers up the Bright Angel Trail from Phantom Ranch when we met a mule train coming down the trail. Customarily, the hikers coming up move to one side of the trail to let the mules go by when the trail is too narrow for both to pass safely. In this case we were standing on the lower side of the trail away from the cliff face so that we were looking up at the mules as they went by. This perspective made the mules and riders appear even larger than normal.

The mule train which was passing us contained a number of people from our bus tour who had decided to ride down to Phantom Ranch and back out again the next day. In the group were Dr. Duane Gish and his wife, Lolly. Dr. Gish is about 5 feet 4 inches tall and was seated on the largest mule I've ever seen. He was wearing a gigantic, black, ten-gallon cowboy hat and his legs were splayed out almost horizontal. He could barely reach the stirrups because his legs were so short. Dr. Gish looked like a miniature version of Hopalong Cassidy on a horse many times too large. He was moaning and groaning from the agony of having already ridden about six miles. He still had three miles to go to get to Phantom Ranch plus another ten miles to get back out of the canyon the next day. Not surprisingly, he still says that this mule ride was one of the worst experiences of his life and that he never, ever wants to ride a mule again.

The trail below the switchbacks flattens out and continues on to the river, which is another two miles away. A steel suspension bridge crosses the river to Phantom Ranch on the other side. Once you get to Phantom Ranch, you are ready for a nice long break. The hamburgers and cokes never before tasted so good. Picnic benches placed strategically under cottonwood trees lend an air of comfort and relaxation. The breeze whistling through the canyon also soothes the jangled nerves. Whether you arrive by foot, raft, or mule, Phantom Ranch is a true oasis in the middle of a desert.

Dr. Duane Gish riding down Bright Angel Trail.

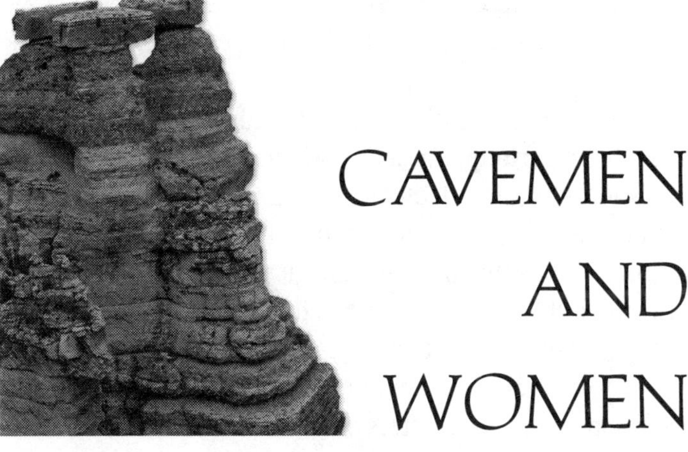

CAVEMEN AND WOMEN

FOR THE FIRST 1 5 YEARS of my involvement with tours to the Grand Canyon, I had only taken the bus tour twice. I have been on the raft twice but have lead backpacking groups ten times. Interestingly, on both of the years I was on the bus it snowed at the south rim, causing great consternation to everyone. Snow, cold temperatures, and wind make it very difficult to hold outdoor lectures on the rim at the start of the trip, and backpackers and rafters find these conditions very uncomfortable and potentially dangerous.

As a professional meteorologist, it has become my duty to forecast the weather in the canyon for the week of our tour each year. Under most circumstances, it's not really possible to accurately forecast the weather more than about three days ahead; but occasionally, when a warm weather pattern dominates the western United States, it is possible to predict with some degree of certainty that the weather will likely be hot and dry for the entire week of the tour. However, because we purposely schedule our tours in the spring each year, and intense storms can plunge down the West Coast from Alaska unexpectedly, one can never be certain that a brief snowstorm won't occur in the middle of the week.

It is not only my job to notify everyone a few days before the trip what the weather is likely to be but to update all the participants at our orientation briefing in Phoenix and at the rim lectures on Sunday afternoon at the start of the tour. I have found after making these forecasts for many years that no one really acts on my forecast ahead of time, but when I forecast bad weather which actually occurs, I get blamed for it.

More attention is paid to my forecast the day before the backpackers and rafters descend into the canyon, however. At the orientation, I typically strip to a pair of shorts and a T-shirt to give my weather briefing if the weather appears to be hotter than normal for the week. If it appears to be colder than normal, I put on a heavy coat, hat, and gloves. These theatrics are intended to get the attention of the backpackers and rafters. They have the option to take all of their extra clothes, tent, and stoves with them if the weather looks bad. On the other hand, they can leave some of their equipment behind in storage if the weather looks good. Of course, these decisions are based on how confident I am in my forecast and how confident the participants are in me.

In all the years of making these forecasts, on only two occasions have I recommended that the backpackers leave as much equipment behind as they could. On two other trips I have recommended that they take all of their equipment with them because of the likelihood of snow.

In all four cases the forecasts proved to be correct, both for the hot, dry forecast and the cold, wet forecast. In all other cases, I have equivocated and suggested they carry extra clothing to be on the safe side, since I couldn't be certain about the weather for the week. In most of these cases the weather was better than expected.

In the two cases when it snowed, I was traveling on the bus. This happenstance has led to the expectation that if I decide to ride the bus, it will snow at the Grand Canyon during the tour. To insure good weather, I have been encouraged not to take the bus but, rather, participate in the raft trip. Of course, none of these attempts to avoid snow in the Grand Canyon really works. The best remedy is to just blame the weatherman!

Even though I had accurately forecast the weather conditions the year it snowed on the backpackers and rained on the rafters, I was apparently discussed nightly at the evening devotionals. During the Victory Banquet at the end of the tour, when each group is requested to contribute a skit, I was serenaded with songs and poems describing the manner in which the weatherman should be slowly roasted over an open fire or hung in effigy.

During the year of the blizzard of 1990 in the canyon, Don Barber was the backpack leader for the Cottonwood Creek group. Don had considerable experience as wrangler and backpacker from his days as director of several Christian camps. However, he had never experienced leading a group of 16 backpackers into such a snowstorm. On Sunday evening when we reached our rooms at Maswick Lodge at Grand Canyon Village, it had begun to snow lightly. When we awoke in the morning six inches of snow was on the ground at the south rim and more was falling.

Past experience told me that as the group descended into the canyon the snow would turn to rain at lower, warmer elevations and the storm would slowly weaken during the week. But, this didn't reduce the impact of watching 16 backpackers disappear into the gloom as they departed the bus carrying their packs toward the trail head.

Would they be okay? Was it sensible to allow them to proceed?

When Don and his group reached the edge of the canyon where the trail descended into the void below, the visibility was obscured by clouds and snow. The magnificent view of the canyon normally seen from this vantage point was limited to about ten feet of white surface ahead and snowflakes falling from above. No one had traversed the trail since the snow began so it appeared as a pristine layer of cotton covering the rocks and shrubs. Only a slight depression and more spacing between the trees hinted at where the trail was located.

Don is an experienced backpacker, so following the trail was not a major problem, but the footing for his group was a big concern. In places, the trail was quite steep and carrying backpacks could have caused some to easily slip and fall. At the top of the Coconino sandstone where the cliff is vertical the trail twists and turns precipitously downward. On this day the view of 400 feet or more vertical drop to the rocks below did not frighten the party of backpackers because of the poor visibility. However, the white, fuzzy unknown beyond the edge caused considerable uneasiness.

The group worked its way slowly down the incline, walking in Don's footprints as he broke trail. Fortunately, the fresh snow had fallen on dry ground and no ice was present below the snow to make the descent even more treacherous. Some in the party were becoming concerned during the downward trek that the snow might not stop and they would be camping in a blizzard. It crossed some minds that they might even have to endure a week of subzero conditions and need to be rescued. Don assured them that as they descended the temperature would warm above freezing and the snow would turn to rain. Wonderful! Setting up camp in cold rain is always so much fun.

It wasn't until they reached the Supai group at about

2,000 feet below the rim that they ran out of snow and the trail was no longer covered with white. The trail conditions had slowly changed from more than six inches of snow to no snow and then to red mud. Although the precipitation had turned to cold rain and, if anything, had become heavier, the visibility was a little better; but they were still in clouds.

As they moved farther away from the south rim and more toward Horseshoe Mesa, which extended along a ridge into the main canyon, the wind began to increase. The rain began to soak into the group's clothing and the wind had a bite to it. Don was becoming concerned that some in the group could experience hypothermia in these conditions. Setting up camp in the rain would not only be unpleasant, but also difficult, particularly for cooking dinner.

He decided to stop for lunch in a protected area between some rocks and discuss with the group what their options might be for the night. Some of the group were thrilled at the challenge of this camping experience, but a few were somewhat frightened and uncertain about what night would bring. Don told the group that their campsite was on top of Horseshoe Mesa, which is very exposed to the elements. The wind typically blows across Horseshoe Mesa strongly and in this weather would be very uncomfortable. Because of the weather, he was considering finding an alternative camp site which was more protected. Unfortunately, this would place the camp farther from the toilet, but he thought the group would probably appreciate more respite from the wind and weather.

One possibility was to camp in an old abandoned stone building with no roof near the junction where the Grandview Trail spits into the Hance Creek and Cottonwood Trails. Another was to camp among the few trees which exist on Horseshoe Mesa. A third was to crawl into one of the mines or caves in the area. The group agreed that a cave or mine would be preferable. Don said that the park service only allows camping in designated areas in the park, but because of the weather conditions, he felt they might understand.

After a quick snack, the group shouldered their packs and began the last mile and a half into camp. Not long after they started down the trail again, a lonely figure appeared in the gloom ahead. As the figure took shape they could see the uniform of a park ranger with his "Smokey the Bear" hat and heavy raingear. The ranger halted the group with a puzzled look on his face. "Where in the world did you all come from?" he asked.

Don replied for the group, "We came down from the rim heading for Cottonwood Creek."

"Boy, you sure picked a great day to hike the canyon," he said. "Where do you plan to spend the night?"

"Well, we have a camping permit for Horseshoe Mesa tonight, but we were thinking of spending the night in the old mine or one of the caves. Do you think we could get in out of the weather?"

After a moment the ranger replied, "We never let anyone camp in any of the mines or caves because of the historical nature of the sites and the deterioration you will cause by staying there. However, because the weather is so miserable and dangerous today, I'll give you permission to camp in the Cave of the Domes this one time. It's on the west side of Horseshoe Mesa just under the rim. But, you'll have to promise to pick up all your trash and leave it in good condition. I think you'll be safer in the cave than out on the mesa. Besides, if you get into trouble with the rain and cold tonight, it'll be me who has to come out and rescue you."

"Thanks," Don said. "We appreciate your understanding. I know where the cave is and we'll leave it better than we found it. By the way, what are you doing out here?"

"That's my job. When the weather gets bad is when you'll find us rangers out and about. Few people get into trouble when the weather's good. So we get to hike the canyon when it snows or rains or when the temperature is over a hundred degrees. Nice job, huh?"

"And here I thought you guys spent most of your time on the front porch with your feet up on the rail looking over the edge of the canyon," Don said.

"Nope. I wish it were that easy. Well, take care going down the trail and I'll check on you tomorrow morning. By the way, watch the trail going into the cave. It's probably pretty muddy along the cliff right now and it's a long drop over the edge."

"We will," Don said. "Thanks for your help. Okay, everybody. We've got about an hour to get to the cave. Let's head on down the trail, and watch your step. I don't want anybody getting hurt now, after we've already gotten past the worst part."

The group slowly moved off behind Don. The wind seemed to be getting stronger and the temperature was dropping again. Don noticed that the hikers seemed to be huddling closer together now. He was pleased with their performance. Only one person had done much complaining and even he was good-natured about most of it. The three women in the group had worked like troopers. All of them had been well prepared with raingear and had carefully worked their way down through the snow and mud without any serious mishaps. It looked like all the written instructions before the trip and the final verbal instruction had paid off. However, Don was thinking, "If Vardiman ever asks me to lead another group into a snowstorm, he's crazy. Next time, the weatherman gets to lead the group when the weather turns bad."

About 45 minutes later Don led the group past the old, abandoned, stone building and out onto the mesa. He took the west loop toward the Cave of the Domes.

He noticed that the wind was gusting up to 40 knots or more and he was glad for the promise of camping in the cave for the night. One concern he had was that he wouldn't be able to recognize the final turnoff to the cave. If there had been snow as far down in elevation as Horseshoe Mesa he was sure he wouldn't have been able to find it, but even in the rain and fog it was going to be difficult.

Don saw what appeared to be the correct branch in the trail. It headed downhill to the west and looked familiar, but there are a lot of similar gullies on the top of Horseshoe Mesa. He hesitated a moment and the next member of the group bumped into him. Before he caused a traffic jam, he decided to try it. It took about 50 feet down the path before he was confident that this was the right trail. After about 200 yards he came to the edge of the mesa and the trail dipped over a rocky outcrop and ran along the cliff. Don stopped and waited for the entire group to catch up. When the last straggler arrived, he briefed everyone on how slippery this ledge could be and to be extremely careful climbing down.

The group inched along the drop-off and listened as the wind whistled against the rocks and shrubs near the edge. Suddenly, a swirl of wind caught the group and nearly swept two of them over the ledge. Don yelled through the gale to hold onto each other and help the two back onto the trail. One of the women was barely clutching onto a small tree with one hand and digging one toe into a rock crevice when her husband scooped her up and dragged her back onto the trail. She was still trying to catch her breath when another gust of wind threatened to tear the entire group from the ledge.

Don yelled back to the group, "When the wind dies again, move quickly ahead and get into the cave entrance. It'll be less windy just ahead!" Don moved deliberately across the narrow rock ledge and stood to one side helping each member of the group over the final obstacle into the cave.

As the group gathered in the dark just inside the cave entrance they could hear the wind outside tearing at the mouth of the cave trying one last time to suck them to their death. Nobody said anything for a moment. After a few seconds, Fred, unbidden, began to pray out loud. "Lord, thank you for saving us from the wind. Thanks for guiding our steps through the snow. Thank you for sending us the park ranger. Thank you for giving Don the knowledge to guide us to this cave and the safety it provides. Father, we are grateful for your love and care to us. We love you. Amen." And the whole group echoed, "Amen!"

Don pulled a flashlight out of his pack and counted the group. "One, 2, 3, 4 . . . 15, 16," Don said out loud. "All here, safe and sound. Okay, let me tell you a little about this cave and we'll get set up for the night. This is a 'dry cave.' That means it doesn't have any water running through it anymore."

"Thank God," Gloria said. "I've had enough water for one day."

"Well, you won't get any wetter in here," Don said. "But, you could get very muddy. The floor and walls of the cave are very dusty. With all the water you've got on you from the rain, if you touch anything, you'll really get muddy. I suggest you not place anything on the floor for a while until you dry off. If you can't wait that long or must take your pack off, try to find your ground cloth and put it down on the floor before you sit or lay anything down. Oh, by the way, there are areas of the cave which have considerable amounts of bat guano. Check out where you sit. Men, you can have that room over there, and women, you can set up camp in here. If you need to use the restroom, you'll have to brave the elements outside. I would wait a little while for the wind to die down, however. It's about 5:00 p.m. We'll have devotions about 6:30 p.m."

It took about two hours for the group to get their sleeping areas established in the dark and to cook supper. The temperature in the cave was about 65°F. This would be a very cool respite to the normal outdoor temperature in the high 80s this time of the year, but today it was comfortably warm compared to the outdoor temperature of about 40°F. Most members of the group had changed clothes to avoid the wet cuffs, collars, and sleeves soaked by rain pelting the exposed parts of their bodies. The cave looked like a laundry when a casual flashlight beam was pointed around the rooms. Drying clothes hung from every available nook and outcrop in both rooms.

When it appeared that everyone had finished supper and was relaxing, Don called the group into the larger of the two chambers near the entrance to the cave. He placed a bright lantern which distributed light in all directions from the middle of the room. It is forbidden to build campfires in Grand Canyon National Park and that would be doubly true inside this cave. Even if one wanted to build a fire in the canyon, it would be difficult to find enough firewood to burn, even if it were a dry day. The few trees that grow in the canyon don't produce much deadwood because they remain so small. The lantern didn't produce much warmth, but it did brighten up the room and make it cheery.

As the group assembled, the wind could still be heard gusting near the entrance. It was still raining and the sound of falling water tinkled through the cave. Fortunately, near the mouth the entrance sloped away so that no water actually flowed into the cave.

Don called on Roy, a member of the group who had demonstrated some musical talent earlier in the day, to lead in singing. Using song sheets Don had brought with him, Roy led the group in "This is the Day," "His Name is Wonderful," and "Majesty," songs frequently used in the canyon. One of the most enjoyable experiences of a backpacking trip is gathering together after dinner and singing. Normally, the group camps in a side canyon near a stream so that the songs echo off the walls, competing with the frogs croaking nearby. However, in the cave, the sound was amplified much greater than normal and it sounded almost like the Mormon Tabernacle Choir practicing. Thanks to the cave's acoustics, even the quieter members of the group could be heard contributing to the rich, full harmony.

After the rigors of the day, these songs of praise to the Lord had an effect on each camper's heart. With little prompting, several members of the group expressed their appreciation to the Lord for His protection during the day and offered testimonies to His goodness. Don gave a short devotion on the Children of Israel camping in the wilderness and then led in a period of prayer.

For the technical presentation Don decided to talk about cavemen. He used the Cave of the Domes and the snowstorm as an illustration of what conditions may have been like during the Ice Age. As Don made various points in his presentation the shadows from his arms waved on the walls behind him.

Some of the information he shared pointed out that when the flood in Genesis came to an end and Noah and his family had disembarked from the ark, some of the residual effects of the flood continued for many years. During the events of the flood, magma, which flowed to the surface in volcanoes and from the ocean floor along submarine ridges, released great amounts of heat, which probably left the oceans of the world somewhat warmer than they are today. These warm oceans evaporated large quantities of moisture, which continued to fall as rain in tropical regions and snow in the polar regions for several

Don Barber describing the conditions during the Ice Age in the Cave of the Domes.

hundred years after the flood.

Noah's descendants multiplied rapidly on the earth and moved from the mountains of Ararat to the Tigris-Euphrates Valley. When they refused to migrate over the earth as God had commanded them, and when they decided to build a tower to worship the stars and flaunt their pride, God had to forcibly disperse them over the earth by confounding their language.

Many of the peoples moved to the Nile River Valley in Egypt and into China on their way to the Americas. Some traveled into northern Europe and others into Africa. During these migrations, as snow was building up on the continents in the polar regions, water was being removed from the oceans by evaporation. The ocean levels were reduced by 400–600 feet according to some estimates. This allowed land bridges to form between continents, which are widely separated today.

Between Asia and North America, one major land bridge formed across the Bering Strait. Many migrations of peoples occurred across this land bridge, taking people of Asian descent into the Americas. Even today, a noticeable similarity of facial features between some Chinese, Eskimo, and Native American cultures is evident.

In polar regions where emigrants settled near ice and snow, caves have been found where people lived to avoid the elements. During the Ice Age which followed the flood, building materials were hard to acquire in polar regions. It was relatively easy for small groups of people to live in caves and stay out of the rain, snow, and cold. In addition, protection from wild animals was generally easier in a cave.

Many cave cultures occurred in more northerly latitudes, which were stormy a large amount of the time. The food was limited to meat from animal kills. Fresh fruits and vegetables were uncommon and bones from many of these cultures exhibited rickets. This disease is due to a lack of vitamin D. The bones tended to become bent and thick. It is likely that these people also experienced a lot of arthritis.

Finds of cavemen were originally interpreted as examples of early stages in the evolution of man. Many of the images shown in museums show a thick-browed, stooped family of Neanderthals. Those pictured appear stupid and are characterized as having a low IQ. Today, however, cavemen are not as often viewed as exemplifying these traits. Some of the environmental effects are beginning to be recognized. Cavemen are now seen as "people who lived in caves" by some analysts. Artifacts have been found which show that Neanderthals buried their dead, cared for their elderly and infirm, employed agriculture, music, and weapons, and possessed items of religious significance. They were fully human people groups living in harsh conditions.

Don Barber's backpacking group to the Grand Canyon in the snowstorm of 1990 had the opportunity to experience first hand what it was like to live as a caveman. Not only did they have to trudge through the snow and cold, they were forced to live at least one night in a cave. After this experience, I'm sure this group of backpackers has a much greater appreciation for the conditions through which some of our ancestors survived.

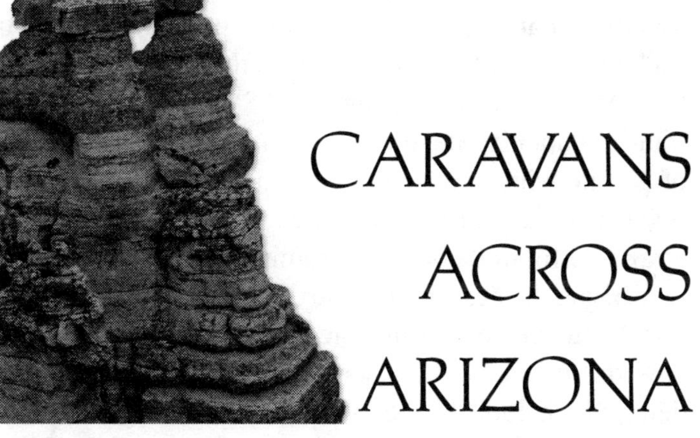

CARAVANS ACROSS ARIZONA

FOR THE FIRST FEW YEARS our trips to the Grand Canyon were designed exclusively for graduate student instruction. Dr. Steve Austin typically drove his car to the Grand Canyon with two or three students, camped in the park, and backpacked for several days. When I first participated on a trip in 1983, the size of the group had swelled to about 15 students and we needed five cars to hold all the passengers and luggage.

One of the benefits of a smaller group is the close fellowship and direct communication possible among participants. Even the leader-teacher, Dr. Austin, soon became known as and addressed by his first name. However, with five cars, the ten-hour trip from San Diego on the coast of California to the canyon in the high deserts of Arizona didn't permit much communication between Steve and the remainder of the group. Although to novices the desert appears an unlikely teaching tool, to a geologist this wasteland is viewed as the best possible place to teach geology. The rock formations are completely exposed to view and are not covered by vegetation. To travel ten hours without an opportunity to comment on the scenery was unacceptable to Steve. So, he arranged for citizen band (CB) radios to be temporarily installed in each vehicle for the journey across the desert.

As we traveled on Interstate 8 from San Diego en route to Phoenix, Steve was able to expound on the shield of granite which covered the Laguna Mountains. As we proceeded, large, round boulders which dotted the chaparral-clad foothills became prominent until, as the highway began the descent into the desert, they were jumbled together to create a formidable barrier between the coastal environs behind and the stark desert ahead. These boulders, which look like they have been dumped from a giant's bag of marbles, scattered and piled at random, give evidence, Steve pointed out, of a recent earth-altering flood. The boulders are large chunks of granite which have exfoliated the outer covering by weathering action and become rounded. Because many of them sit on the very tops of the local hills, they would not remain there for millions of years, given the frequency and intensity of earthquakes common to the Southern California area.

Dr. Steve Austin lectures about granite rocks on the way to the Grand Canyon.

They are a direct testimony to a short period of time since their formation.

Steve also talked of desert varnish and the evidence it provides for recent earth movements. Desert varnish is the dark coating which, with time, accumulates on rocks and boulders from particles and chemicals in the rain and air. The longer a surface is exposed to the elements, the thicker and darker the coating becomes. When driving through a recent road cut, it is easy to see the lighter surfaces where excavations and rockwork have been done. Sometimes these new surfaces, which have been exposed only for a few years, will appear white or light gray or red next to the darkened older rock nearby. Recent landslides and rockfalls also appear lighter. Later, we would see rock art on boulders and cliffs created by Indians over the past few thousand years. This rock art is pecked with a sharp rock into the desert varnish by the Anasazi and other Indian tribes of the desert Southwest. Various animals like antelope and deer appear on the rocks in various shades, depending on how long ago they were made. The darker the object, the longer it has existed.

When we reached the main desert floor near the Salton Sea, Steve began to talk of the Grand Canyon. The deserts throughout the Southwest are relatively flat with sharp, narrow mountain ranges poking into the sky along the horizon. It appears that the desert floor in many places is the result of massive flooding and sedimentation from past catastrophic events. Near the mountains, gigantic alluvial fans spread out on top of this flat desert floor as a result of more recent erosion and transport of sediment down smaller canyons. Steve believes that when the Grand Canyon was formed several hundred years after the flood, it was the result of a catastrophic failure of a natural dam upstream from where the canyon is now located. The sudden, ripping, colossal release of about 1,000 cubic miles of water and sediment into the Salton Sea area resulted.

If the sediment from the carving of the canyon had been carried to the ocean through the Gulf of California slowly over millions of years, it should be observed easily near the continental boundary off the west coast of Mexico. However, no such alluvial fan of sediments is observed on the ocean floor in this location. Consequently, he believes the sediments were deposited in a depression where the Salton Sea and the Anza Borrego Desert are located in southeastern California and southwestern Arizona. Core drillings in these locations have found some 18,000 vertical feet of sediments which have the same mineral characteristics as those rocks found in the Grand Canyon.

Steve presented similar topics over the CB radio as the caravan traveled across Arizona on its way to the canyon. Because of the length of some of the lectures and responses by students, the radio was kept active throughout the day. It is likely that channel 18 on the CB radio was unavailable to truckers or other users for 50 miles in either direction of our caravan as we traveled along. Instead of the familiar CB language heard on the radio like, "Have you got your ears on, Charlie?" or "Keep the shiny side up," truckers in southern Arizona were treated to terms like, "orogenic synclines" and "plate tectonics." Service stations along the freeway which routinely monitor the CB radio network probably received more information on geology than they ever wanted to hear.

After traveling all day, we finally arrived at the Grand Canyon, where we set up camp in Mather Campground. The temperature at the south rim around Easter time is at or below freezing at night. This makes for cold mornings and dressing quickly. However, the groups in those days were generally students who were willing to put up with the inconvenience of camping for the benefit of inexpensive accommodations.

The next year a larger number of people, many of

whom were not students, wanted to go with us. For transportation, we used an old yellow school bus which had no air conditioning. Naturally, that was one of the years when the temperature each afternoon exceeded 100°F. It took us about 14 hours to reach the canyon that year, partially because of a blowout of one of the rear tires with no spare on board. When we arrived about 10 p.m. after a long, hot day, we had to set up tents by headlight while supper was prepared for the entire group over a kerosene campstove. Dave McQueen prepared a large kettle of his homemade concoction which became known as "igneous chili" because of its resemblance to glowing, red lava with dark chunks in it. It was hot both to the touch and the taste. For the less hardy, he also cooked up some "metamorphic chili" and for the greenhorns, he had some "sedimentary chili." Needless to say, the night was also punctuated with sounds and aromas of the musical fruit.

I remember at least two particularly pleasant experiences of camping at Mather Campground. The first was the hot showers available to campers for one dollar. After spending a week backpacking in the canyon and then returning to Mather, the first desire is always to bathe in water as hot as possible and remove the grime. Except for cold sponge baths in the shallow creeks which flow through the side canyons or a dip in the 40°F Colorado River at the bottom of the canyon, nine miles and at least a day's hike away from Mather, no one takes a bath for five days. The bathhouse at Mather Campground provides a total of about two dozen (half for men and half for women) individual shower stalls which provide water at a temperature of at least 120°F and a pressure that will tear the skin off your body. After taking a shower at Mather following a week of backpacking in the canyon, I felt cleaner and fresher than at any other time in my life. This was probably due to the fact that I had shed at least two layers of skin in the high-velocity flow from the shower and now exhibited a bright pink complexion free of all worldly contamination. No shower at any motel in which we've stayed on our tours compares to the showers at Mather Campground — particularly those cold, wimpy showers in the hotels we now use in Flagstaff, Arizona.

The second pleasant experience was wrapping myself around a large, juicy T-bone steak at the restaurant at Bright Angel Lodge near the top of Bright Angel Trail. When you survive a week of eating the equivalent of Top Ramon soup and hiking miles vertically and horizontally, your body craves large portions of meat and potatoes. By 1985 we had shed the discomfort of the old yellow school bus for a comfortable Greyhound bus. However, to save money for our students, we were still camping at Mather Campground. This slide into the lap of luxury was beginning to produce side effects. After taking our showers we couldn't face one more night of Top Ramon before turning into our cold sleeping bags.

On the spur of the moment, we decided to inquire of the bus driver if he would be willing to drive us about three miles over to the Grand Canyon Village for a steak dinner. He agreed and 30 minutes later we found our party all seated around a group of tables in the Bright Angel Lodge Restaurant overlooking the Grand Canyon at sunset and chowing down on 16-ounce T-bone steaks. This was the genesis of the Victory Banquet we now hold at the end of each tour. I remember this setting as one of the most enjoyable experiences of my life. A beautiful view out the window, sweet fellowship inside a warm, cozy room, and some of the best food I've ever eaten. The Lord is good!

For those of you who have taken a bus or car tour of the Grand Canyon but have not participated in one of the more strenuous activities, such as backpacking or rafting, you will probably never appreciate the significance of hot showers in the hotel at the end of the week nor the

Victory Banquet. The banquet is not simply a time of fellowship and reflection on the week, but for some it is the first stage in recovery from involuntary fasting. Please excuse some of our more ravenous guests if they initially drool and use their hands at the buffet table. We customarily call on the backpackers to lead the charge to the food, because if we don't they may riot and do someone mischief!

We've added three components to our Victory Banquet we didn't have in the early years which have come to be almost as enjoyable as the good food and fellowship. We now have singing, testimonies, and presentation of research projects. Some of the best singing this side of heaven occurs at our Victory Banquets. Each of the separate groups have been singing together in the canyon and on the bus. When we all get back together for the final activities, everyone is comfortable with each other and just sings his heart out to the Lord and the group. Maybe I get overly sentimental at the end of a tour because of the physical and emotional exertion, but I find singing on our tours to be the high point of my spiritual life each year.

We also have each backpack group, the raft group, and the bus group offer a skit, testimony, or song as part of our festivities at the Victory Banquet. We've had songs and skits about "Moleskins," "Fill My Cup, Lord," and, of course, "Doom to the Weatherman." Occasionally a personal testimony is given which relates how an experience on the trip has changed a person's life. The aggregate of these testimonies and activities has given me great joy as I remember the part our tours have played in people's lives.

The last part of our Victory Banquet has been devoted to a brief presentation of research we are doing at the Grand Canyon and other places. Many of our participants on the Grand Canyon tours in recent years have helped fund the analysis of rock samples to show the discordance of radioisotope dates from different dating techniques, and the production of various videos.

The Victory Banquet, which had its start as a steak dinner following one of our early backpacking trips for graduate students, has blossomed into one of the main features of not only the Grand Canyon tour but also is now the concluding group activity for the Mount St. Helens tour, the Yellowstone tour, and the Israel tour, offered for the first time in 1998. It's amazing how the Lord can use a simple event to His glory.

A similar development has occurred on the Grand Canyon tour as a whole. After progressing from a few cars, to an old yellow school bus, to a Greyhound bus, the tour today typically includes two or three large-window touring buses with adjustable seats and a video system. Between 20 and 30 backpackers hike the canyon on each tour, about 40 rafters float the Colorado for five or six days, and a bus tour of about 50 people visits the Grand Canyon and surrounding parks. We no longer camp in Mather Campground, eat "igneous chili," or have our skin nearly torn off in the Mather showers but rather stay mostly in three or four-star hotels.

We now originate the tour in Phoenix to shorten the bus drive to the canyon and have a three-hour presentation about the Grand Canyon to get everyone oriented. On the way to the canyon, all members of the tour are treated to a large-screen IMAX movie of the Grand Canyon. The tour now caters to the general public rather than graduate students. However, tour fees are maintained at a level which makes it possible for several graduate students to receive stipends to help cover their expenses. Some of the more advanced students may also be used as leaders, particularly on the backpacking groups. In such a capacity they incur no cost to participate and may have an opportunity to collect data for their thesis research.

The Grand Canyon tour has progressed from a caravan of cars across Arizona to a professional quality tour which has ministered to over 2,000 people since its inception. However, the main goal of the tour has not changed — to demonstrate to those who are open the evidence for the flood as revealed at the Grand Canyon. Where before only graduate students had the opportunity, now the general public can experience the canyon.

THE CANYON BY BUS

BUS TOURS, BY THEIR NATURE, tend to offer less dramatic experiences than the raft or backpacking groups encounter. Few participants on the bus tours come in contact with wild animals or face dangerous circumstances or severe weather conditions. However, several interesting situations have occurred which have not only challenged the spiritual maturity of our group but have also been found to be humorous upon reflection.

Some of the members of our bus tours have physical limitations of one kind or another. Some have high blood pressure or a heart problem and have to watch their activities. Others may have a bad leg or a bad back. One year we were able to take a lady who was confined to a wheel chair. These limitations have not prevented our guests from enjoying most of the activities planned for the bus tour.

Since about 1990 the Grand Canyon tour has begun at a hotel in Phoenix, Arizona, with registration on Friday night followed by an orientation on Saturday morning and a Mexican buffet at noon before heading to the canyon. The lobby of the hotel is like a family reunion on Friday night, as many old friends return for another tour. Many of our guests have taken one of our other tours or have attended one of our conferences around the United States or abroad and know many of us and each other. New guests participating in the Grand Canyon tour for the first time find themselves easily incorporated into this friendly atmosphere.

On Saturday morning one of the first accomplishments is to get all the luggage stacked near the hotel entrance so it can be loaded on the buses during the orientation. For the last few years, we have had three full-size tour buses leaving Phoenix. It's astounding to see how much luggage is required for about 150 guests, including backpacks, boxes of books, folding chairs for guests at the rim on Sunday afternoon, and suitcases. Each bus carries 55 people, so there is typically over 100 pieces of luggage per bus. When it is all piled up in front of the hotel, it looks like the U.S. Army is billeted there.

We've only lost a few pieces of luggage during all the years of the Grand Canyon tour, and those were eventually found. Four boxes of books were lost one year at the hotel in Flagstaff but were eventually returned about six months later. The most humorous incident occurred when dropping off guests at Sky Harbor Airport in Phoenix at the end of a tour in 1994. Caroline Albright was scheduled to fly back to England early Monday morning following the tour, so had placed her suitcase in the cargo hold of her bus to return to the hotel with her on Sunday evening. When she got to the hotel and it didn't show up, she paged Tom Manning, the tour coordinator, at the airport where he was waiting with part of his family for a flight to San Diego. Tom sent his son to look for the suitcase on the curb outside the airport, but he was unable to locate it. Tom called the hotel in Flagstaff to see if it had been left behind. Calls to the concierge at the hotel in Phoenix and to the bus company didn't help.

Finally, just as Tom's flight was about to leave, he called Caroline again at her hotel and was told that her suitcase had just arrived. Apparently, the suitcase had been unloaded from the bus and left standing on the curb outside the airport. Before Tom's son got to the street to look for it, a baggage clerk from the airport had found it and arranged for it to be delivered to the hotel. Since that incident we now have one of our staff remain overnight in Phoenix to handle any last-minute problems for our guests.

Most bus tours contain interesting people and the fellowship is a special part of the tour experience. In fact, the most frequent comment expressed on our survey taken at the end of each tour is how great the fellowship was. We begin each tour with introductions by all participants. On the way from Phoenix to the Grand Canyon, each person is given the opportunity to give a two or three-minute statement about why they are on the tour and to add any special information they wish to share with the entire group. Almost everyone is willing to speak briefly over the intercom. Some are more than willing and give five to ten minutes. It is a great way to get the tour started and find out about our neighbors on the tour.

Tom Manning has introduced a fun reminder for those who tend to be late returning to the bus after a sightseeing activity or other event. He awards a child's play clock to hang around the neck of the latest person returning to the bus. That person gets to wear it until the next time someone is late. This minor but humorous embarrassment reminds us all to be on time and not delay the others. There is usually one person who wears it most often.

The start of each day is begun with a short devotional, singing, and a period of prayer. Typically, the devotional

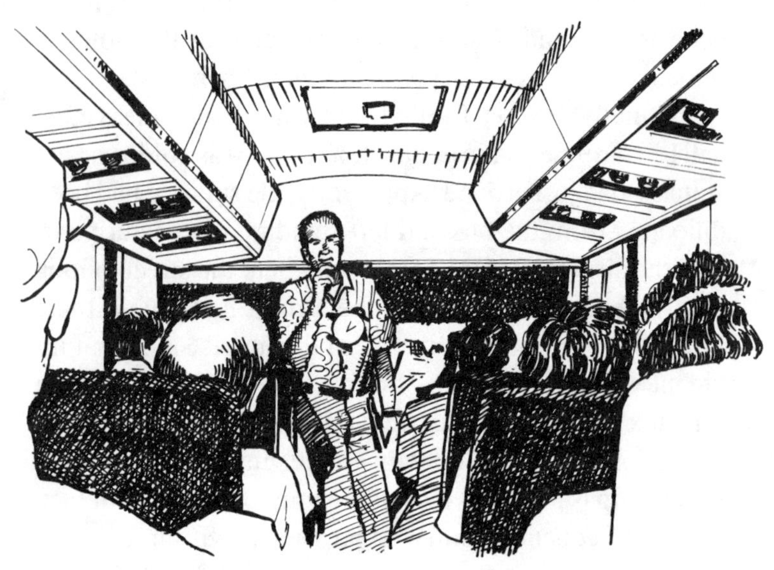

Tom Manning giving instructions on the tour bus.

is given by one of the staff on a topic related to the sights for the day. Occasionally one of the guests is asked to bring a devotional or a testimony. The singing is a special event on our tours. None of us are professionals, but the groups often have excellent singers, and the choruses and hymns really sound great driving through the beautiful scenery often encountered in Arizona.

We schedule our arrival at the Grand Canyon on Saturday afternoon in time to see a 45-minute movie at the IMAX theater before viewing the sunset from Mather Point. The movie gives some of the history of the Grand Canyon including a reenactment of Native American culture before the arrival of the white man. My favorite scenes are the ones filmed from an ultralight airplane flying down into the narrow canyons, along and just above the river, and over the crags and ledges of the canyon. I've often jokingly suggested that we need to create a fourth group on our tours which will fly ultralight aircraft through the canyon. Unfortunately, this is not possible because flight below the rim of the canyon is now forbidden except in the case of an emergency.

After viewing the IMAX film, our tour group travels to Mather Point and views the sunset, if the weather cooperates. Some of our guests have never seen the Grand Canyon before and this first view is always an exciting experience for them. This vast depression in the earth can never be adequately captured on film. The beautiful blue, red, and green colors; shapes of the buttes and monuments; and the incredible magnitude of the canyon itself all lend a special aura to the place.

On Sunday morning we normally attend worship service at Grand Canyon Baptist Church. This is a Southern Baptist Church which meets in the beautiful Shrine of the Ages Chapel. It has a beautiful window on one wall which looks outward to the ponderosa pine forest covering the rim. On most years one of our leaders has been asked to be the morning speaker. Several friends attend this church, including Ron and Sue Clayton who operate the mule concession for the park.

After church all three buses travel out to one of the overlooks on the east end of the Grand Canyon for a short series of minilectures. For the last few years we have been conducting these lectures at an overlook near Desert View Tower. From here the entire group can see both the strata of the Kaibab upwarp and the lower desert to the east where we believe large lakes were impounded before the Grand Canyon was eroded. Several of the tour leaders give short talks about the canyon from this vantage point. In 1987, in addition to the standard technical lectures, Dave McQueen organized a special "lecture" at this point in the program. He coerced several medical doctors who were guests on the tour to dress up in surgical gowns which he had brought along for the occasion and "operate" on a patient in front of the assembled group. He equipped each doctor with standard surgical tools, draped a table with surgical coverings, and even had head lamps for some of them. While the doctors "operated" on the patient, Dave described several symptoms the patient was having, which were couched in geological terms. For the punch line, one of the doctors, identified as Dr. Rock, finally located the problem by pulling a large stone from an "incision" on the patient.

At the end of the minilectures the three buses then head in different directions — the backpackers return to Grand Canyon Village to prepare for their trek into the canyon, the rafters travel to Page, Arizona, for one last night of comfort before embarking on their voyage down the Colorado River, and the bus tour group begins a five-day visit to Zion and Bryce Canyon National Parks and other nearby scenic locations.

Before separating for the remainder of the week, the rafters and bus group have lunch together at the Cameron Trading Post on the way to Page, Arizona. There are two unique features to this stop. First, this is probably one of the best locations for Indian jewelry in Arizona. It has the largest selection of silver, jade, turquoise, and other keepsakes found anywhere. The bus group stops here twice and has the opportunity to look the first time and buy on the return visit. Second, the Cameron Trading Post has the biggest, most delicious taco you will find on the trip. You can order the Navajo Taco, which completely covers a large plate, or you can order half of a Navajo Taco. John Morris likes these tacos so much that he describes most of the geological formations to the bus group in terms of a Navajo Taco. If you order one, however, be careful of the hot sauce.

By the time the bus group finally heads toward Zion

National Park, the people begin to recognize one another and form closer friendships. As we hike along the trails together at Zion and Bryce Canyon and fellowship together on the bus, the bonds become even closer. Many friendships have been developed on our bus tours. Part of the bonding occurs because of the devotionals and singing on the bus. Several of the leaders take turns leading devotionals and the singing, but John Morris is probably best known for his gracious encouragement with old time songs which aren't sung in churches much anymore. He particularly likes songs based on geological terms like rocks, sand, and mountains.

At the end of the week when the rafters and backpackers rejoin the bus tour for our Victory Banquet in Flagstaff, the singing reaches a special crescendo. It may be that the individual groups have become accustomed to the smaller sound of their own group, but when they come together in the larger group, the amplified, enclosed sound of the total group makes an incredible impact. Maybe it's just that practice makes perfect. At any rate, each year I am overwhelmed emotionally when the whole group sings together. I am particularly partial to singing "Majesty" and "How Great Thou Art" at our Victory Banquet.

Prayer on the bus tour also has special meaning. Many people come on our tours who have needs that they can't share easily with friends and loved ones at home. Our tour is a very nonthreatening group of loving Christians from all over the United States and around the world. Sometimes it's easier to share some very deep, personal need with someone you aren't likely to see again than it is with your best friend. We always have people on our tours who reach out in love and concern to someone who has needs and deep hurts. We've had many who've recently lost spouses and loved ones. We've had parents who are concerned for their children. We've had pastors who've been badly treated by their churches. We almost always have a few who are not believers but are searching. Members of the bus tour group almost invariably wrap their arms around those who are hurting and pray for them during the week. Many times these relationships continue for many years after the tour. A few couples have even gotten married because of the acquaintances they've made on our tour.

The bus tour doesn't allow the participants as much time in the Grand Canyon as the rafters or backpackers, but this limitation is compensated for by travel to many other locations near the Grand Canyon. Some of the places visited during the past ten years are: Zion National Park, Bryce Canyon National Park, Lake Powell, Rainbow Bridge, Kodachrome Basin, Petrified Forest, the Painted Desert, Sunset Crater, Meteor Crater, and Walnut Canyon. There are opportunities for short hikes at each of these locations. At some, horseback and helicopter rides can be arranged. For the last few years the entire bus tour has been able to travel on a raft down the Colorado River from near the foot of Glen Canyon Dam to Lees Ferry, where the rafters start their trip. Although only small rapids occur on this stretch of the river, the high canyon walls, Indian petroglyphs, and good fishing give a first-time visitor a real exposure to what "running the river" would be like.

The final events on the last day of our Grand Canyon tour are always bittersweet. After Sunday morning services in Flagstaff, the buses head toward Phoenix via Oak Creek Canyon and Sedona, Arizona. Although Sedona is a typical western tourist town, the scenery in and around the town is anything but typical. The red rocks, which have been eroded, form all kinds of shapes. Oak Creek Canyon contains magnificent scenery. Between sheltering crimson cliffs, pine and oak-shaded glens alternate with grassy meadows as the creek trickles downstream. Driving though this canyon at the end of a week at the Grand Canyon, Zion, and Bryce winds the emotions down so that one can face the thought of returning to worldly cares. One can keep the tranquil image of Oak Creek Canyon tucked away in the recesses of his mind as a refuge to which he can return if present cares become too great.

After lunch on that last day, the return to Phoenix only takes about two hours. The buses drive directly to the airport where most guests take planes home the same day. Sometimes this departure will take our participants by surprise. If you take our tour, I suggest that you prepare yourself for that sudden separation from the group. If you don't, you'll feel like someone pushed you out the front door of his house and closed the door. One moment you are enjoying the remnants of a week of fantastic scenery and fellowship, and the next you are standing alone on the curb of Sky Harbor Airport surrounded by hot, desert air and the noise of hundreds of buses, cars, and planes.

If you want to take a more leisurely return to civilization, stay on the bus and return to the hotel in Phoenix for one last night before returning home. About a third of our guests choose to stay overnight. I've done it, and I highly recommend it.

FLOAT AND BLOAT

MAINLY BECAUSE OF THE QUALITY of the food eaten by the rafters and the ease with which they view the canyon, the portion of our tour which takes rafts down the Colorado River has become known as the "Float and Bloat" contingent. The companies which provide the rafting service typically feed the raft group steak, shrimp, Mexican fajitas, spaghetti, and other incredible feasts as they drift downstream during the week. Even during the day, the rafting companies offer snacks and drinks whenever a guest desires one.

In addition, if one wishes, he need only step off the bus at Lees Ferry below Lake Powell and into the raft, float all the way down the Colorado River to near Lake Mead, climb out of the raft, and then ride in an air-conditioned van out of the canyon. Of course, most of our tour participants are much more active than that and only care to take our raft trip halfway to cut their time and cost in the canyon. The two primary options are for our guests to travel on the raft from Lees Ferry and walk up Bright Angel Trail to Grand Canyon Village at the end of the trip, or to walk down the Bright Angel Trail to meet the raft as it empties for the beginning of their trip and take the van out of the canyon at Lake Mead. Each of these trips is about five days and the cost is about half of that for rafting the entire distance. Unfortunately, those who take the second half miss the wonderful fellowship at the Victory Banquet, but they get to experience several of the best rapids on the river.

During the raft trip there are optional day hikes up side canyons to view geological formations. Some of these day hikes can be quite rigorous. In particular, on the up-river portion of the raft trip, the trek to view the folded strata of the Kaibab upwarp, and, on the down-river portion, the hike up Havasu Canyon to swim in the beautiful blue-green waterfall-pools on the Havasupai Indian Reservation, require fairly good stamina. If one stays only in the raft and floats down the river, he will miss a major portion of the enjoyment of the canyon. So, floating and bloating is really a misnomer, but the backpackers can't help but denigrate the rafters for the apparent luxury they believe the rafters enjoy.

We have sponsored about a dozen raft trips down the Colorado River since the Grand Canyon tour began in the early 1980s. Steve Austin floated the river the first time in 1980 by invitation from Art Chadwick, a biologist with Loma Linda University. Steve had just moved into a new apartment when he received a call from Dr. Chadwick asking if he would like to join the Loma Linda group at 4:00 a.m. the next morning for a trip through the canyon. Because a trip down the Colorado is a once-in-a-lifetime dream for most geologists, Steve immediately said yes, even though it took him several hours of searching to find his equipment in the jumble of his recent move. This raft trip later convinced Steve that a similar experience should eventually become a part of the Grand Canyon tour.

Probably the most significant aspect of the raft trip is the impressive view of the geological strata one experiences on the way through the canyon. As one floats downstream, he drifts past a sequence of rock layers which occur in similar order as if one were to hike down one of the trails. However, in this case the rafter has the opportunity to study them slowly as they go by, unencumbered with the exertion of carrying a pack and hiking long distances. It's amazing how rocks can lose their charm (except for a committed geologist) when one becomes tired and sweaty from physical activity. This doesn't happen on the raft. You can simply lie back and watch as rock layer after rock layer emerges from the canyon ahead, passes slowly alongside the raft, and disappears to the rear.

As you proceed down the canyon these rock layers seem to rise from the earth and loom over you. You are able to see these layers from numerous perspectives as you traverse the canyon. As the river works its way downhill it cuts through the Kaibab upwarp, a mound of rock strata which was folded upward sometime in the past through which the canyon was eroded. The rock strata, which were originally formed in horizontal layers, were tilted upward by the movement of the crust along a line north/south through the park near Desert View Tower. The carving of the canyon allows the rafter to observe these layers inclined upward toward the west as he floats downstream, very much like driving past a large road cut through a mountain.

To be more specific, we teach that the canyon was formed by the catastrophic failure of a natural dam which held back the waters of several large lakes impounded upstream in Arizona, Utah, and Colorado. We believe the evidence is sufficient to show that water impounded

Dr. Steve Austin lecturing to a group of rafters at Nautiloid Canyon on the Colorado River.

upstream in at least two large lakes containing a thousand cubic miles of water, carved the canyon rapidly when a section of the Kaibab upwarp failed. One of these historical lakes, called Hopi Lake, filled the depression now covering northeastern Arizona in the watershed of the Little Colorado River. The Kaibab upwarp forming the dam failed just east of Desert View Tower near the present junction of the Little Colorado and the Colorado Rivers.

Shortly after this event, a second natural dam near Page, Arizona, failed, releasing a second giant lake that filled a depression which now includes Lake Powell. This second lake, called Canyonlands Lake by Dr. Austin, would have been deeper than Lake Powell and would have extended upstream into the Four Corners regions, covering Monument Valley. The Grand Canyon, Marble Canyon, and the Canyon of the Little Colorado formed by the erosive action of water flowing over and through the failure points. The erosion began at the failure point and worked its way upstream. This type of erosion is called "downcutting" and is similar to what is still occurring slowly today at Niagara Falls. The exact mechanism for the initial failure through the Kaibab upwarp to start the flow through the Grand Canyon is still being investigated. The mechanism is thought to be either "overtopping" or "piping" through underground fissures in the strata. Dr. Austin prefers the piping theory because of evidence which has been found for numerous underground caverns and channels in the redwall limestone, in many of which water still flows today.

The topography of the Grand Canyon, with its narrow Inner Gorge and wide, amphitheater-shaped side canyons seems to cry out for massive flows of water in the past which produced rapid erosion, rather than a slow erosion by a trickle of water over a long period of time. The Colorado River exhibits what is called in geologic terminology, a relic landform — one which was formed in the past and has not changed significantly since its formation. We teach that the Grand Canyon was probably carved within a few hundred years after the Genesis flood. Some of the layers would have already hardened into rock, others would have still been unconsolidated and somewhat soft.

In addition to the ease in which the canyon can be viewed by the rafter, one other useful benefit to the raft trip is its convenience for carrying heavy loads into and out of the canyon. The collection of rock specimens for chemical analysis from formations in the canyon was always a challenge until we began the raft trips. Now, when rock samples are collected under permit by Dr. Austin or other associated geologists, they can be carried by the raft and easily transported home to San Diego for analysis.

The largest load we have carried on the rafts, however, in addition to the people and their personal gear, was the equipment needed in 1993 and 1994 to produce the videotape on the geology of the Grand Canyon. We contracted with Jeremiah Films, Inc. to produce a creationist documentary during the 1993 raft trip. Randy Ide, a professional video producer and cameraman, was subcontracted by Jeremiah Films to join the raft trip those years and obtain footage of the canyon, as well as recording interviews and activities for production of the video.

Randy brought with him a $50,000 network production video system which was composed of a Sony Beta camera, a recording deck, a tripod, and batteries. In addition to the primary camera system, Randy had a backup video camera and all of his personal equipment. All of this special equipment, which weighed close to 100 pounds, was no problem to float through the canyon and retrieve when the trip was over. However, when outcrops and interviews needed to be filmed up side canyons away from the river, the transport of the camera system became a major operation.

Steve Tecklenberg, a friend of ICR, volunteered to carry the heavier parts of the camera system to the field locations. Steve is about six and a half feet tall and weighs over 240 pounds. He was able to carry the camera, tripod, and recording deck all by himself. However, even he was challenged by a trek to the 60-mile formation. This was a site about five miles up a side canyon and over 2,000 feet above the elevation of the river. The site is significant because of the rock material of which it is composed and the evidence it contains for rapid, catastrophic formation. Because of the remoteness of this site, it is likely that we have packed a video camera farther than anyone else into the back country of the Grand Canyon to produce a video.

Because of his efforts for ICR on this project, Steve Tecklenberg has become known by the 1993 and 1994 rafters as "Packmule." When Steve Tecklenberg and his father, Paul, again floated the river a couple of years later in 1996, he wore a T-shirt with the words "Packmule" printed on it. His father wore a T-shirt with the words "Father of Packmule" imprinted on his. Since Steve didn't have camera equipment to carry around that year, he volunteered to pack a hammer, chisel, and rock samples, which Andrew Snelling collected from layers and ledges high above the river.

Because in 1993, less than one hour after the rafts launched from Lees Ferry, the $50,000 camera quit working, it took two years to acquire the footage necessary for our video production. One of the circuit boards on the camera malfunctioned and no repair was possible in the field. Randy Ide was forced to document the activities with his backup camera, which was of insufficient quality to be used for the production. The humor of the situation was not apparent to the group at the time. Here was a professional video producer, equipped with the best video system money could buy and provided with a floating platform on the Colorado River for ten days and a "mule" to carry his equipment, reduced to recording lectures and hikes like any other tourist with a camera purchased at a chain store.

Randy returned in 1994 to successfully complete the project. His work can be seen in the video, *Grand Canyon: Monument to the Flood.* The cover of this video can be easily identified by the beautiful picture on the jacket of a group of ICR rafters heading off downstream in a raft with the canyon dwarfing the scene. This documentary features five creationist geologists (Steve Austin, John Morris, Andrew Snelling, Van Burbach, and Kurt Wise) on location, discussing features of the canyon which support its recent, catastrophic formation rather than an ancient, uniformitarian process. A major portion of the production cost was covered by generous donations from the 1994 raft group. This successful video has justified all the effort and expense which went into its production.

Of course, to many people the geology of the Grand Canyon is secondary to the thrill of riding the rapids on the Colorado River. The Colorado River between Lees Ferry and Lake Mead contains some of the best white water in the world. Thousands of people raft, kayak, or boat the Colorado each summer simply for the thrill of challenging the rapids.

John Wesley Powell was the first white man to lead an expedition on the Colorado River through the Grand Canyon. In 1869 Powell traversed the canyon in specially built wooden boats. He traveled the entire 200 miles of the Grand Canyon without prior knowledge of the rapids or waterfalls which lay ahead. Prior to this, even Native Ameicans who knew the area avoided the river, recognizing the canyon's formidable, insurmountable cliffs. Powell's intent was to map this wild section of the new western territories for the U.S. Geological Survey. Each turn in the river, each sound of rushing water ahead, could spell disaster for his men. The Inner Gorge in particular, with its narrow vertical walls and dark recesses, seemed to invite catastrophe. The next rapids could be a waterfall, for all they knew. Would the river simply disappear into the bowels of the earth, taking the entire group with it to oblivion?

Powell started with over a dozen men, but three were killed during the exploration of the canyon. Two gave up to walk out just before the final stretch of river. They were never seen again. Of course, the river had not been dammed when Powell made his run, and his boats were much more likely to swamp or overturn than those used today. A re-enactment of Powell's famous trip on the Colorado River may be seen at the IMAX theater near Grand Canyon Village.

Today's Colorado River runner typically rides in either a large rubber raft, a kayak, or a newly designed boat similar to John Wesley Powell's. Each of these designs allows for a much safer passage through the rapids. Today's raft groups float the Colorado on large rubber rafts provided by one of several groups in Arizona. They are typically made from Army surplus pontoon boats which have been modified to hold large quantities of food, equipment, and people. They are powered by 75 horsepower outboard motors. Each raft normally holds about 15 riders, including the boatman, so the group is composed of two or three rafts floating down the river together.

The raft companies provide almost all necessities for each person. They provide and prepare all the meals; provide sleeping bags, cots, and tents; and set up bathroom facilities at each campsite along the river. Each passenger is expected to assist in loading and unloading the raft at each stop. The group typically forms a "fire line" and passes equipment and food from the raft to the campsite and back again each day. This group activity quickly helps mold the participants into a team.

As the rafts float down the river, the temperature changes abruptly from sometimes over 100 degrees to below freezing. When the rafts are in the sunshine on a hot day, the heat can become almost unbearable, but when in the shade on a cold day, it can become very chilly. Whether the day is cold or hot, the river is always cold, having been described as "liquid ice." The water in the canyon comes from Lake Powell and is extremely frigid all year round because it comes from melting snow in Colorado, Utah, New Mexico, and Arizona.

The Colorado River typically runs green when no recent storms have washed muddy brown water from upstream. Because of the cold, green water, trout fishing is excellent in most of the canyon. During the 1995 raft trip I was able to catch about a half-dozen trout, one of which was 21 inches in length. Even when recent storms have muddied the Colorado, the first 80-mile stretch from Lee's Ferry to the Little Colorado River is still clear and excellent for fishing. However, almost any recent rain in eastern Arizona will cause the Little Colorado River to run brown. When it enters the main Colorado just east of Desert View Tower, the two flows will run parallel for only a short distance before the entire river turns brown. Fishing under these conditions is poor. Before boarding the rafts we always make one last stop at a sporting goods store for rafters to purchase fishing licenses and equipment.

When running the river, each person in the group wears a rain suit and a life vest. The group is instructed in safety procedures should anyone be swept off the raft into the current. If a person falls into the river, he is not to fight the river but to relax, keep his head above the water, and point his feet downstream. This reduces the likelihood of a luckless rafter striking his head against a rock. Within a few minutes a person overboard will pass through the rapid and float into the calm water downstream and the boatmen will quickly fish anyone out of the river who may have fallen overboard. Of course, this interval of time may seem like an eternity to the victim because of the extremely cold temperatures and the fear of rushing water all around.

We have had only one passenger fall overboard in the dozen trips we have taken into the canyon. That person was Steve Tecklenberg, whose restraining strap slipped while riding "the horn" through Lava Chuar Rapid. Steve was rescued within a minute or so of clearing the rapid, cold and wet but unharmed — and loving every minute of it. During most of the rapids the boatman will allow people to ride on the horn of the outriggers — the pointed front end of the rubber tubes which support the edges of the raft. There are straps wrapped around the tubes to hold onto and this is the best place to experience

Pontoon raft with the tour group navigating one of the rapids in the Grand Canyon.

the thrill of riding the rapids. However, during some of the heavier rapids, like Crystal, Lava Falls, and Sockdolager, the boatman may require all riders to sit inboard. The food and equipment are all stored in the center of the raft and are covered with a tarp to prevent them from getting wet. Around this large pile is a narrow seat on which most of the rafters can sit. There are straps to hold onto and the ride is much gentler.

When entering a large rapid, the boatman will attempt to position the raft just to one side of the main flow so that the raft will pass through the rapid and not get "hung up" in the large "hole" that develops just downstream from the underwater obstacle which causes the rapid. If the boatman is successful, the raft will fall off the wall of water upstream, drift down one side of the "hole," and continue up the downstream wave of water. This not only gets the raft through the rapid safely but produces a thrill for the riders very much like a roller coaster.

In 1995 I attempted to document the transit through Sockdolager Rapid with my 35 mm camera. I took a series of photos of two rafters who were riding "the horn." I photographed them from my position in the center of the boat. As we approached the rapid, I took a picture of Linda and Jerry leaning forward, eagerly anticipating the rapid. My second picture was taken after we had dropped off the wall of water into the "hole" and were just beginning to bounce upward on the downstream wave. The picture shows "the horn" bent upward and a curl of water beginning to fall over them. My third picture, taken about a second later, shows nothing but a wall of water between them and me.

More than a dozen large rapids and many dozen smaller ones exist in the Grand Canyon. These rapids occur mostly where side canyons enter the main river, having brought rocks and boulders downstream and dumping a "rock garden" in the river. This partial blockage of the river causes the water to be slightly dammed and form turbulent flow over the boulders. In some locations underwater sills of harder rock which cross the river at right angles to the flow will produce small waterfalls and turbulent flow.

Daily and seasonal variations in the flow of the river caused by releases from Lake Powell and the accumulation of sand in the channel will regularly change the characteristics of each rapid. The boatmen must rely on their experience from previous runs through each rapid and a "reading of the water" to determine the safest path through. Of course, the boatmen want the participants to enjoy their ride down the canyon, but they don't want to lose riders into the river or upset a raft. It is not uncommon for a boatman to lose a propeller when running a rapid, but rafts are seldom upset. Each raft carries several spare propellers and even an extra motor should they strike a rock on the way through a rapid.

Because of the thrilling experiences and new perspectives gained in the canyon, our raft groups have strongly bonded over the years. Several couples have met and married after participating in one of our raft trips. Numerous couples have renewed marriage relationships. Many others have testified to the importance of these trips in developing and consolidating their views on creation and the flood.

Probably one of the most interesting stories to come from a trip to the canyon was shared by a rafter from one of our early trips. Jack Rhinehart was flying on a United Airlines flight from Los Angeles to Denver when they passed over the Grand Canyon. It is not uncommon for pilots to make an "S turn" over the canyon to allow the passengers to see the features of the Inner Gorge and the side canyons. However, on this day the pilot was supplementing the view with a discussion of how the canyon had probably been carved by a catastrophic flow of water through a break in the Kaibab upwarp near Desert View Towers. He explained how the event may have occurred only a few thousand years ago, not over millions of years as is commonly taught.

Jack recognized this presentation from the lectures he had heard while on a Grand Canyon raft trip five years before. When he arrived in Denver he waited for the other passengers to disembark and stuck his head in the cockpit to inquire of the pilot where he had learned this information. When the pilot turned to greet Jack, he was Wes Eastgate, one of the participants on the same raft trip Jack had taken. They renewed an old friendship by swapping familiar stories from one of their favorite adventures.

Grand Canyon raft trips are more than just adventure and fun. They encourage new friendships. They develop new appreciation for the truthfulness of God's Word. Enthusiasm for Christian fellowship and witnessing to the world occur naturally in this environment. If you haven't had an adventure in your life recently, maybe this adventure is for you.

THE TANNER DEATH MARCH

DURING SEVERAL TOURS to the Grand Canyon the weather has been extremely hot, to the point that backpackers have not needed to carry tents or heavy clothing. However, in 1987 the daytime temperature reached unusually high levels and backpacking became almost unbearable. Dr. John Morris led one of the groups of 16 backpackers that year down the Tanner Trail near Desert View Tower in the eastern section of the Grand Canyon. David Rush and Walter Barnhart assisted John on this trip. Because of the heat and the lack of water on this trail it became known as the Tanner Death March.

The group knew that they would be "dry camping" on the first night and would not have water until they reached the river at the end of two days. Each of the hikers carried four quarts of water with plenty of electrolyte additives in the form of Gookinade, lemonade, and Gatorade. However, the extremely high temperatures were not anticipated, so the hot, dusty trail became a real challenge to the cohesiveness of the group. At the rim John started the group out with a challenge that no one would make any complaints all week. These trips are typically not only challenging physically and intellectually but also emotionally and spiritually. Since we are a Christian organization, we desire to provide an experience in the canyon which provides an opportunity for participants to grow in all these domains. We view the backpacking trips somewhat like a Christian "Outward Bound" experience. This week became a real laboratory opportunity for this expectation.

After being dropped off by bus at the trailhead, the group set off, descending the trail through the layers of Kaibab limestone, Toroweap formation, Coconino sandstone, hermit shale, and Supai group to the top of the redwall limestone, where they spent the night. The group was well into their second quart of water by the time they reached camp. They conserved as much water as they could during supper and the morning meals. However, when they started down the trail on the second day, most had little more than a quart of water to last the day. Unfortunately, the second day was even hotter than the first, partly because they were lower in the canyon, where the daytime temperature exceeded 120°F on some portions of the trail.

After they dropped below the redwall limestone to the Tonto Platform, the temperature was high, but not as high as it was to become below the Tapeats sandstone. On the Tanner Trail, as opposed to other trails in the canyon, the Tapeats sandstone lies on top of the Cardenas basalt and Dox siltstone, rather than Vishnu schist and Zoroaster granite. These lower sedimentary layers are tilted upward from the north side of the canyon and extend part way up the Tanner Trail. This is one of the few places the Cardenas basalt and Dox siltstone can be studied on the south side of the river in the canyon. Creationist geologists have speculated for years how these layers fit into the flood model.

Many creationists assume that the sedimentary rock layers began to accumulate above the hard crystalline basement rock on the Great Unconformity at the end of the flood. In the Grand Canyon the Great Unconformity occurs at the interface between the Vishnu schist and the Tapeats sandstone. The Vishnu schist was apparently planed off by the fast-moving waters of the flood, leaving a relatively flat surface on which the flood sediments began to accumulate as the flow of water began to slow and drop its sediments. In eastern Grand Canyon, however, the inclined layers of Dox siltstone, Shinumu quartzite, Hakati shale, Bass limestone, and Cardenas basalt don't appear to fit into this picture.

First, because the layers are inclined, they would appear to have been formed before the Genesis flood or, if not then, during the initial bursts of the flood. Second, these layers have been reported to contain fossils of a plant that grows in shallow oceans. The most likely time these layers would have formed before the Genesis flood would have been on the third day of creation when God separated the continents from the oceans. There seems to be no other geological events described in the Bible which are sufficiently catastrophic to produce these layers between creation and the Genesis flood. God created some plants on the third day and the process of separating the continents from the oceans on this day would likely have done considerable geological work and produced sediments. It is possible that these layers did not require some catastrophic process to form but represent deposition offshore from the well-watered pre-flood continents.

These layers do not contain any marine animals, which would be expected if they were formed during the flood. However, creationists have not yet studied them sufficiently to identify the time and process of their formation with any certainty.

As the Tanner backpackers made their way across the Supai group below the redwall limestone, they found plenty of worm burrows, invertebrate "hash," and some evidence of trilobite tracks. As they moved into the Cardenas basalt and Dox siltstone, no evidence of any fossils was found. In fact, few plants even grow in this layer today. These layers are composed of red and black loosely-consolidated material which easily erodes and forms small gravel and dust. The Tanner Trail traverses these layers on the east side of a north-south canyon so that the sun strikes these dark layers almost perpendicularly in the afternoon, creating extreme temperatures. The backpacking group trudged on and on for several long miles.

By midafternoon the group lost almost all interest in geology and paleontology as they made their way to the Colorado River. Stumbling over the never-ending and never-changing Dox siltstone sapped every bit of interest and attention. By this time no one had much, if any, water left and everyone was walking in almost dead silence, anticipating the cold, refreshing river water for drinking and wading. The temperature was at least 120°F and dust caked the boots, faces, and arms of every hiker. The dark

Dr. John Morris leading the Tanner Death March.

red dust gave them the appearance of Anasazi Indians carrying backpacks. Their bleary eyes betrayed the near desperate plight of this band of intrepid explorers.

After nearly three miles of hot, dusty hiking across the Cardenas basalt and Dox siltstone, the Tanner group finally caught a glimpse of the Colorado. As they quickened their pace, they began to realize that the river was not the bright green color they were expecting. In fact, it appeared to be a dirty, brown color. When they finally reached it, they were appalled to find that the river was flowing like thick, chocolate pudding. No one could drink this water, even though they were literally dying of thirst. John immediately broke out the Catadyne filters for purifying drinking water and began to pump water into a canteen. In less than two strokes of the pump, the filter was clogged up with silt, and water stopped flowing from the outlet tube.

John immediately realized that they would be unable to filter the river water this way and jokingly stated, "We're all going to die!" One spunky member of the group promptly reminded their leader of the trail head challenge "not to complain all week" and followed up by suggesting to John that he build a small settling basin on the river bank and resume using the filter when most of the water had clarified. While John built the settling basin, most of the group removed their shoes and began to wade in the river to cool off and refresh their feet. However, no one remained in the river for more than about two minutes because the water was so cold and so painful to their suffering feet. After about 30 minutes John resumed pumping, this time from the settling basin, and was able to slowly fill several canteens with fresh water by continually disassembling and cleaning the filter.

As the sun descended behind the canyon walls to the west and the temperature began to drop, the group finally came out of their lethargy, worked to repair blisters on their feet, and continued to pump water. Although they were no longer in danger of heat exhaustion, they soon realized that pumping water from the river was so time consuming that they needed to find another source of water. John suggested that they join up a day early with the raft group by hiking upstream to Lava Falls where the raft group would be spending the night. The raft had a large pumping system and could supply them with all the water they needed.

Since it was still daylight, the group headed eastward over the ridge toward the site where the raft was scheduled to spend the night. On the way they encountered the largest rattlesnake ever seen by any of our hiking groups in the canyon. Rattlesnakes in the canyon have taken on a pink color to match the red sediments washed downstream from the Supai group. They look just like timber rattlers, except for their color. This particular snake was over five feet long and very fat. Color variation in rattlesnakes is part of the adaptation to environmental conditions they encounter, not due to evolution. Rattlesnakes apparently have the natural variability built into their genes which allows them to take on different colorations. Snakes with a pink coloration have a greater chance of surviving in the Grand Canyon than green ones. If pink Grand Canyon rattlers were transported to an environment where green coloration was favorable to their survival, the descendants of the pink rattlers which tended to have a more greenish tint would eventually outnumber the pinkish rattlers.

The same adaptability to black or white coloration has been found to be true for the peppered moth in England. The increase in the number of black peppered moths during the industrial revolution was at first ascribed to evolution. The disappearance of white moths was found to be a response to the added smoke in the air and black deposits on surfaces. The natural predators of the moth were able to see the white moths more easily than they could black moths in the sooty locations. When the environmental conditions were later cleaned up significantly, the number of white moths increased again. This was no evolutionary change, only a statistical adaptation to the environmental conditions.

Just before dark the Tanner group climbed the last ridge on their way to Lava Falls; ahead they could see the rafts tied up at the campsite on the other side of the river. John yelled down the hill and attracted the rafters' attention. Soon the rafts had crossed the river to pick up the hikers. Even better, they brought a bucket full of cold, juicy oranges, as well as fresh water. Not long after, the entire group of rafters and backpackers sat down to a fantastic spaghetti dinner. If you are going to have a tough day hiking in the canyon, the best way to end the day is to meet up with the raft group on the river for one of their famous meals.

The next morning the Tanner group joined the raft group for a hike up Lava Canyon to see the folded strata, which were formed in this part of the canyon when the Kaibab Plateau was upwarped. After this hike and because of the tough two days coming down the Tanner Trail, the Tanner group had to spend considerable time that evening working on their feet. Many had large blisters and sore feet. Moleskin was applied liberally. Because of the amount of moleskin used by the group and the great singing the Tanner group exhibited that night and at the Victory Banquet on the following Saturday evening, it was given the nickname "The Moleskin Choir." The Tanner Group had originally taken the name "The Tanner Troubadours," when they discovered that the group had an unusually good set of voices. They practiced their four-part harmony for the raft group that night and sang an especially effective version of "When I Survey the Wondrous Cross." John offered a devotional on Psalm 22, bringing a great day to a close with the Bible's prophetic account of Christ's endurance under ultimate suffering.

The next day the raft group floated the Tanner group through Lava Falls and back down to the Tanner Trail, taking the grateful hikers with them. After being supplied with fresh lemonade and plenty of water, the Tanner group headed back up the trail. Following an uneventful two-day hike, the Tanner group made it to the top of the canyon, 5,000 feet above and ten miles away. One woman had injured her knee and remained with the rafters to Phantom Ranch, where she took a mule ride to the rim. Such problems are a continual threat, but God has always answered our prayers for health and safety.

Although no one died or was permanently injured by the experience, this hike is still known as the Tanner Death March. This title is probably overstated, but when the leader of such an experience becomes our president, he is entitled to some latitude.

THE MOLE

EVOLUTIONISTS ARE OFTEN puzzled by creationists. Even while ardently attacking what they believe as incredible stupidity and religious bigotry, they have a hard time understanding what motivates us. Two anti-creationist organizations, The National Center for Science Education (NCSE) and the American Humanist Association (AHA), in particular, closely follow our activities in order to "protect" the general public from what they label as "the pseudoscience of creationism." It is common practice for correspondents with NCSE and AHA to attend public meetings held across the United States and report on activities conducted and statements made by creationists. Typically, after attending a meeting where evolution was refuted and creationism supported, they write detailed, if not fully accurate, articles which ridicule the statements or even the evidence which was presented. They become particularly incensed when biblical apologetics is used to support creation or the flood.

We welcome these hard-core critics to our presentations, debates, and museum, as long as they are not disruptive. We find that the arguments we present, particularly when accompanied by the Word of God, occasionally have an impact, even on some who are fully convinced of evolution and long geological ages.

As far as we know, however, no skeptic has participated in our backpacking groups before or since the June 1985 backpacking trip down the Bright Angel Trail. We became aware, after the fact, that a "mole" had joined our tour when an article by Phil Smith, one of our participants, appeared in the 1987 issue of *Creation/Evolution*, a publication of AHA. Phil was a Ph.D. candidate in anthropology at the University of California at Los Angeles when he decided to join our tour as part of his research on creationism. On his application for the trip, he indicated that he was interested in learning about creation science, that he was studying evolution and creation science as competing belief systems, that he hoped to pick up some knowledge of geology, and that he wanted to see how the Grand Canyon could be used as an argument for creation science.

This trip was unusual in several respects. Not only did we unknowingly have someone joining us who intended to report on our activities in a critical manner, but the trip occurred in June, which is always hot in the canyon. This year the temperature reached a record 148°F in the deep canyon and the group assisted many less-prepared hikers along the way who were suffering from heat stroke. We've never had another backpacking trip in the summer because of the extreme heat experienced on this trip. The group also had a number of participants who have been increasingly involved with our ministry over the years. In addition to John Morris and Dave McQueen, who shared the leadership of the group, Russell Humphreys, a physicist at Los Alamos National Labora-

Dr. John Morris leading a discussion at Indian Gardens during the oppressive heat of 1985.

tory, later an ICR adjunct faculty member, and biologist Frank Sherwin, later on staff, were also part of the group.

Phil was not disruptive to the activities of the trip because he had come to observe and report, not to try to refute the teaching being done. He remained relatively quiet during the tour and appeared to be one of the more introverted members of the group. Most of the others assumed that he was a creationist, or at least receptive to creationist teaching, because of his quiet demeanor. In fact, Phil was quietly documenting statements, activities, and events for use in his future article and thesis. To his credit, he did not make any false claims or try to act out a part. He avoided stating his own conclusions regarding creation science and did not make any claims about his religious beliefs.

When called upon by John Morris to give a summary of the explanation of the canyon's origin from the "creationist flood theory" during an evening "campfire" meeting, which included some additional guests met on the trail, Phil demurred and mumbled something to the effect that he was still trying to absorb these lessons and it might be better if someone more confident answered. He later wrote, "I couldn't bring myself to present the creationist explanation as if I believed it, especially to strangers (though it turned out that our guests were sympathetic to creationism). Later, when someone in our group asked me why I declined to answer, I said that I have great difficulty speaking in public, which is also true."

At another time on Sunday morning during a worship time together, during which Dave McQueen, who led in a communion service, asked Phil to lead the group in prayer, he once again declined, as he also did when the communion elements were passed. He stated that, "No one seemed to resent my shyness and my admitted unfamiliarity with doctrine, but everyone else offered prayer freely, easily, and often. Once I was asked to which church I belonged. I replied that my wife still attended Catholic church. My questioners muttered condolences and did not press the matter."

Due to the excessive heat and jeopardy to the health of the hikers, several planned activities had to be canceled or postponed until dusk. Resting in the shade of cactus or yucca plants doesn't sound very pleasant, but the creationist discussions were rich. Russell Humphreys and Frank Sherwin, who are experts on magnetism and parasitology, respectively, talked incessantly about the decay of the earth's magnetic field and the original, created purpose of parasites. These discussions educated the group in a special way and gave Phil even more material for his critique.

Although Phil did not create any great difficulty by his participation on the trip, it is somewhat disconcerting to acknowledge that we were not more discerning of his true state and, in fact, had a spy in our midst. From this experience and others, we have come to realize that our statements and activities are always under scrutiny. Of course, we have always known that God is constantly observing us, but we have now come to appreciate just how open we are to criticism by the world. The article Phil wrote about the trip probably confirmed for the evolutionists what they suspected creationists do when they visit the Grand Canyon. Phil concluded, "The main emphasis of this 'geology field course' was religious: seeing in the Grand Canyon a warning to heed God's word and accept Christ before the coming destruction of the world, communicating this to fellow hikers, and fellowship with our own group of believers." He disparaged the amount of time that was spent on devotionals, Bible study, and witnessing. He belittled the geological arguments, rejected the catastrophist interpretations, and caricatured the personalities of the group.

However, I believe Phil also did all creationists a great favor. When I read his description of the trip, the people on it, and the events which occurred, I recognized this trip as typical of many of the trips I've been on myself. Phil described the experience through the eyes of an unbeliever who does not accept the basic reliability of Scripture, God as Creator, and motivations which come from the Holy Spirit; but he reported the trip in a manner which was fairly evenhanded and consistent with a recounting of the events I have received from John Morris, David McQueen, and others. I don't believe Phil's article showed creationists in a bad light. In fact, I believe the article is actually a testimony to the integrity of creationists and the manner in which they conduct themselves before the world. Phil may have been affected more than he realizes by the sincerity and goodwill of the participants in the 1985 tour to the Grand Canyon. I sense that he actually enjoyed the fellowship among these strange, naive creationists!

Phil Smith and many other evolutionists are offended by the use of the Bible, the catastrophist arguments for the formation of the Grand Canyon, and the emphasis on witnessing. But, if the main criticism we receive is using the Grand Canyon as a warning to heed God's Word and to accept Christ before the coming destruction of the world, then I will accept that criticism gratefully. We are doing the job we were called to do. I am thankful that the message came through so clearly.

Sometimes we get discouraged because we believe no one is listening to our message and we think we need to yell it louder. We sometimes come to that conclusion because we don't see many accepting the evidence. However, we are not responsible for the acceptance of the message, only for giving it out. When someone like Phil Smith so clearly understands the message and still doesn't accept it, we need to recognize, that we are doing the job we were called to do. It's up to the Holy Spirit to deal with his heart. Maybe someday, Phil will make his decision to accept the Lord based on the seed that was planted and what he heard and experienced during the 1985 trip to the Grand Canyon.

BEARS IN THE NIGHT

OCCASIONALLY WHILE ON one of our trips some of our tour participants have trouble of one kind or another. They may receive bad news from home or have some type of medical problem while hiking or traveling with the group. Fortunately, we have been able to care for all emergencies in one way or another. In some cases the person is transported to a local hospital or we share a prayer need with the group and the entire bus or hiking group prays for that specific need.

Once a ranger had to descend to Horseshoe Mesa with a message for a member of our hiking group, Dr. Ben Aaron, the surgeon who removed the bullet from president Ronald Reagan. Dr. Aaron had to quickly return to Washington D.C. on an urgent matter. The group bid a sorrowful goodbye as he began his solitary hike to the rim after only one night in the canyon. We are prepared for most emergencies with first aid and CPR training and we carry a first aid kit for minor scrapes and bruises. Leaders are also instructed in procedures for obtaining help for more serious injuries. Helicopters can be summoned to retrieve persons from the canyon in the case of snake bite, heat exhaustion, broken bones, or heart attacks. However, a helicopter ride out of the canyon is expensive and only serious incidents merit the cost involved.

Generally, the group leader determines if a circumstance is serious enough to send for help. He will also provide supplies or minor medications to persons who have complaints. In most cases, the problems relate to blisters and sore feet. If the person is not accustomed to using moleskin, the leader may help ease the pain by fitting a portion to a hiker's foot. In some cases, however, the group leader may not be able to suggest a solution to the problem or may himself be the source of the difficulty. On this particular backpacking trip, both situations occurred.

In 1992 Walter Barnhart and I led a group of 16 backpackers down the Grandview Trail to Horseshoe Mesa and then on to Cottonwood Creek. We had with us four couples, four single women, and two single men. Of the couples, Paul and Mary were to be frustrated on the way into the canyon. Mary would experience a medical condition which kept us all puzzled for two days. This was particularly difficult for Paul, as Mary had agreed to come on this backpacking trip to please him, who, it turned out, had made several trips to the top of Mount Ararat in search of Noah's ark. He wanted her to enjoy some of the remote experiences in which he participated, but her condition was spoiling it.

Four of the singles were young freshmen college students, one of whom was my daughter, Kelly, and another was her friend Sharon Rybka. Two of the other college students had been brought on the trip by Sarah Whitlaw, a 70-year-old family friend from Salem, Oregon. Sarah was one of those wonderful older adults who continues to be active into her senior years and can run circles around the rest of us. She ministers to young adults by teaching and encouraging them in the things of the Lord. In this case, she offered to bring two of them, Eric and Susan, on our tour of the Grand Canyon. Eric was a tall, handsome young artist who was studying to become a concert pianist. Susan was a bright, young athlete who had already competed in downhill skiing championships in hopes of being selected for the American ski team to the Olympics.

After the usual preliminaries of getting to the canyon, having a final pack inspection on Sunday afternoon, and being driven to the trail head on Monday morning, we started down Grandview Trail about 9:30 a.m. It was a beautiful, clear day as we edged over the lip and into the canyon. We worked our way down the first 1,000 feet of steep trail and reached a shady spot at the bottom of the Coconino sandstone where the trail crosses a small fault zone. We normally stop for lunch here before tackling the hot, flat trail across the Supai group. However, we try not to stay too long in this spot because it is often a bit cool, and everyone's muscles begin to stiffen up and get sore. No one had complained about their packs or their feet yet, but Bill, a small hiker from Houston, had taken a bad spill on a slick part of the trail not long before we stopped. His walking stick had slipped off a rock and he had fallen to his knees with the full weight of his pack. He immediately got up and continued walking, so we didn't discover how badly he had scraped his knees until later in the week when he had difficulty walking back up the trail.

After a pleasant lunch of peanut butter cups, trail mix, and fruit, we continued down the trail out onto the red, sandy Supai group. These layers are red because of the iron oxide they contain. Unlike the Coconino sandstone layers above, which exhibit evidence that they were laid down under rapidly moving water, the Supai group appears to have been laid down more slowly. As we understand it, the Genesis flood was a complex of many temporal high energy events. Often the process was unthinkably dynamic, but sometimes the water temporarily calmed, allowing fine sediments to settle. Ripple marks are found in abundance on rock layers throughout the Supai group. These ripple marks are the types of features you might find on the bottom of a shallow lake or around a beach today, except these marks are permanently embedded in solid rock. Apparently, the marks were formed when the sand was soft and was then covered by new sand, preserving the features until the sand hardened into rock. The red color of iron oxide was either produced while the layer was exposed briefly to the air at warm temperatures or the sand turned red in hot water as it was deposited. In either case, some process caused the iron which was present to be combined with oxygen, similar to the rusting of an iron bridge.

When we have two leaders on a backpacking group, I typically ask the other leader to take the lead and I bring up the rear. This allows me to help encourage those who may be lingering or having some problem. Besides, this way I can blame my slow pace on that of the others. Walter, who navigates the canyon like an antelope, was up front heading toward Horseshoe Mesa, where we planned to spend the night. We were about two hours from our campsite and the group was beginning to spread out along the trail. I noticed that Paul and Mary had slowly dropped back to a position just ahead of me, and Paul was having to more frequently help his wife down steep places in the trail and up the other side. After several such episodes, I asked Mary if she was feeling ill. She replied that her stomach was very upset and that she was dizzy. I suggested we stop to let her rest until she felt better. She gratefully sat down and began to express her apologies for slow-ing down the group. I told her not to worry about it. We had plenty of time to get into camp before dark and that she could take as much time as she needed.

Most of the group ahead had stopped about a quarter of a mile down the trail when Walt noticed we weren't keeping up. After we rested about 10 minutes, we again started down the trail and came upon the front part of the group just getting ready to leave. I told Walt that Mary was not feeling well and that if we had to rest again, he and the others could go on into camp. We would probably arrive late, but would be there before dark. While I was talking with Walt, Mary sat down again to rest and didn't feel like moving again for 20 minutes this time. When we again starting hiking she only went about a hundred yards when she said she couldn't go any farther and wanted a helicopter to take her out of the canyon. I told her that it would be impossible to get a helicopter this late in the day and, besides, it would have to land on Horseshoe Mesa where we were going to spend the night. If she could just work her way into camp slowly during the remainder of the afternoon, we would send someone out for a helicopter tomorrow morning, if she still needed one. I suggested that she would probably feel better in the morning and would likely be able to continue on. It was not uncommon for people to get a slight case of the flu from traveling or contact with others while on the tour. It normally lasts less than 24 hours. Besides, the cost to get a helicopter into the canyon could range between $500 and $1,000.

Over the next three hours, we were able to slowly walk a little at a time the remaining mile into camp. When Walt arrived in camp earlier with the main portion of the group, he sent several of the stronger members back to help carry Mary's pack while he and a few of the others hiked down to Miner's Spring at the base of the redwall limestone to get extra water for the night. Everyone, including Mary, finally arrived in camp by sundown and began to set up tents and prepare dinner.

During devotions that evening Mary requested prayer that she would be okay tomorrow, but as of then she was feeling fine. Her nausea had gone away and she was as good as new. We all felt greatly relieved and encouraged her to get a good night's sleep.

All of the adults went to bed immediately after devotions, but the four college students decided the night was still young, so they all gathered in one of their tents and played cards until after midnight. As they played, they began to hear night noises and tried to identify some of the sounds. One of the noises sounded suspiciously like a bear. One of Susan's hobbies was hunting bears in the northern Sierra Nevada, but she said she doubted if any bears lived in the Grand Canyon.

We awoke to a beautiful sunrise on Horseshoe Mesa the next morning. The scene from near the edge of our campsite is one of my favorite places on the entire earth. The view toward the east from the top of the redwall limestone layer is magnificent. Below the 1,000-foot drop-off from the redwall lies Hance Creek, flowing northward to meet the Colorado River through a cleft in the Tapeats sandstone. The Tonto Platform at the top of the Tapeats sandstone layer is covered with bluish-purple blackbush, buck brush, and blooming flowers in the spring. Darker patches of green shrubs and an occasional light-green cottonwood tree stretches along the edges of the creek. To the northeast, one can see glimpses of the Colorado River in the darker Inner Gorge winding its way southwestward toward the foot of Horseshoe Mesa. As the rising sun inches over the ridge near Desert View Tower about ten miles away, its rays are almost blinding. Behind, the upright cleat at the rear of the horseshoe from which Horseshoe Mesa gets its nam, rises about one hundred feet vertically, exuding its red, Supai coloration in the bright beams of the sun. These scenes mixed with the sounds of waking birds and the smell of pinion pine and sage await only the first smells of brewing coffee to be complete.

Since our hike to Cottonwood Creek, about two miles down the redwall and toward the north, would only take about three hours, we didn't push to get an early start. Most of the adults began to stir by 7:00 a.m., but the college students had to be kick-started after their late night of cards. Not long after everyone was awake, Betty, one of the single college students, walked over to my tent and asked where she could find an electrical outlet. I dumbly turned around to see her peeking through her messy hair, carrying a hair dryer.

"I'm sorry," I said, "but the nearest outlet is five miles or more away near the rim of the canyon."

"You've got to be kidding!" she said. "You mean I carried this thing all the way down here for nothing?"

"I'm afraid so," I replied. "You'll just have to use a comb."

She walked slowly back to her campsite and sat dejectedly in the door of her tent, looking as if the world had come to an end. After a few minutes she began to work on her hair, and before long had tied it in a ponytail and looked as good as new. A few hardhearted souls offered to loan her an extension cord or reported that they had found an electrical outlet from time to time on the rest of the trip, but Betty seemed oblivious to their offers of help. During the remainder of the trip she had the nicest hairdo and best makeup of anyone in the group.

By about 9:30 a.m. we were on the trail working our way down a very steep initial part of the cliff followed by about a half mile of little, round, marble-like rocks on a steep incline. We made good time over the steep part, but by the time the way flattened out, Mary was again having a very difficult time negotiating the irregular parts of the trail. She had stopped at a convenient rock and was sitting very still when I approached her to see how she was doing.

"I want a helicopter, now," she said. "I don't feel at all well and I don't think I can go on. I'm dizzy again and feel like I'm going to vomit at any moment." Her husband, Paul, reluctantly agreed.

I told them that I would be willing to send Walt out to get a helicopter now if that's what they wanted, but Mary would either have to climb back up to the top of Horseshoe Mesa to be rescued or would have to continue on into a site near our camp for the night at Cottonwood Creek. The terrain where we were currently located was too steep for a helicopter to reach her. I then began to ask her if she was on any medication or if she had any recent illness or medical condition I should be aware of. All our participants fill out a medical history form as part of the application process so that we can screen any potential health problems. She had not indicated any serious health problems, so both she and I were at a loss to explain her condition. If she had the flu, she should not be exhibiting intermittent dizziness and nausea for such a long period of time.

After reciting her recent medical history, which included only minor illnesses, she mentioned in passing that she had just recently been to see her eye doctor and had been given a new prescription for her glasses. A bell went off in my head. I asked if she was wearing a pair of glasses with a new prescription. She replied that she was and that for the first time she had been prescribed bifocals.

Bingo! That was it. "Mary," I said. "You are seasick! Seasick in the desert! You are not accustomed to your new prescription and looking up and down as you hike over rocks and down cliffs is causing you to constantly shift your focus from the top frame of your lenses to the lower one. Your new prescription for bifocals is causing you to get sick. I purchased a new pair of bifocals about two years ago and it took me a week or more to get accustomed to them. I kept stepping off of curbs and misjudging the distance to the street below or tripping over steps. If you only got yours last week, I'm almost certain they are the cause of your discomfort."

"You've got to be kidding!" she said. "I didn't even think about my glasses. What should I do?"

"How well can you see without your glasses?" I asked.

"Not too bad," she said. "Things up close are a little fuzzy, but I can see okay beyond about three feet."

"Good," I said. "Just take off your glasses for the rest of the hike and I think you'll be okay. When you get into camp you can use them, but try to hike the trail without them. It's the constant looking up and down that's making you sick. I recommend that you hike on into Cottonwood. If you still don't feel well this evening, we'll consider a helicopter for you tomorrow. But I expect you'll start feeling better within a half hour or so."

After she rested for about a half-hour, Mary started down the trail without her glasses and made it into camp without further incident. By the time she reached camp, she was feeling fine. She and Paul placed their tent above the remainder of the camp with their backs to the cliff and surveyed the valley below them. They felt on top of the world for the rest of the trip. That night we all rested better knowing that Mary was okay and we wouldn't have to request a helicopter rescue.

I've always enjoyed camping at Cottonwood Creek. It is located next to the stream where a small trickle of water gurgles near the campsite. Our tents were located on a small platform between the creek and a 30-foot high wall of Tapeats sandstone. The site is protected from the wind except when it decides to blow up or down the canyon. Several bathing sites in the creek are within a short walking distance downstream, if one can endure sitting in cold water up to his chest. The creek water is not really as cold as the river water, but it's still bracingly cold. I've only been able to do it on the hottest days.

In the spring this creek always has hundreds, if not thousands, of small frogs in it. At nighttime, just about time for devotions or bed, they begin to croak. When so many frogs begin to croak, it sets up a tremendous din, especially in a narrow canyon. Strangely, about nine or ten o'clock at night, they will all quit croaking at the same moment. The camp will suddenly become silent and the quiet becomes very eerie.

On the second night at Cottonwood Creek, Eric announced that he was moving his tent away from the main group to a clearing about 50 yards away. When asked why, he stated that he had at first thought the sound he was hearing late at night was bears growling near the camp. But, last night he had gotten up and tracked the sound to my tent. He claimed that either a bear had taken up residence in my tent or I was the loudest snorer he had ever heard. Susan confirmed his suspicions and announced that she and my daughter, Kelly, and Sharon would be moving their tents in another direction, also farther from camp. After all, she ought to know a bear when she heard it. She had hunted and killed several bears in her lifetime.

I told them that I didn't snore! They must be mistaken. There probably were bears in the woods, and if they moved away from the group they risked being dragged off and eaten by them. This didn't seem to deter them and one of the adults even chimed in that he didn't believe bears lived in the canyon. I told him, "What do you know? I'm the leader of this group and if I tell you there are bears in the woods, then there probably are bears in the woods!"

"But, there aren't any woods in the Grand Canyon," he retorted.

The remainder of the week was relatively uneventful. With only minor problems we all made it out of the canyon. Mary had no more difficulties, but Bill had a hard time climbing up the trail. We found that his knees had swollen from the fall he had taken earlier in the week, and we had to wrap his legs with Ace wrap to help support him and ease the pain. However, by going slowly he was able to make it to the top and rejoice at the Victory Banquet with the group. We always celebrate the survival of the groups each year on the last night of our tour and thank the Lord for His mercy.

On Sunday the bus left Flagstaff, Arizona, after a church service held in the hotel and headed toward Sedona, Arizona, for a brief lunch stop on the way to Phoenix. Shortly after leaving Flagstaff this year, Tom Ellingham, who was one of the single men on the Cottonwood Creek backpack group asked if he might use the video system on the bus to show a short segment of a video. He said he had taped much of our hike in the canyon and had a two-minute segment he thought the entire bus of hikers and

Kelly and Sharon discover the source of the bear noises.

backpackers might like to see. I told him it was okay with me if he had it queued up ready to see.

I took the tape to the front of the bus and started the video. Before I could return to my seat to view what he had taped, I could hear noises coming from the video system which sounded like a bear growling. As I sat down, the entire bus was laughing and pointing to the TV monitors and me. There on the screens was a close-up image of me sleeping on the ground with my hat over my face, my head resting on a bedroll, in the shade of the Tapeats sandstone at the Cottonwood Creek campsite. It was in the middle of the afternoon and I was snoring up a storm! At that point I had no option but to admit that I snored and there were no bears in the canyon. Prima facie evidence such as had been offered could not be refuted.

THE GREAT ANASAZI SIPAPU

WHEN NOAH AND HIS family disembarked from the ark on the mountains of Ararat only a few thousand years ago, it didn't take them long to begin repopulating the earth. Noah's three sons and their wives began having children very shortly after the flood.

Noah would have been unable to initially have a peaceful family life after leaving the ark. The mountains of Ararat reach a maximum altitude of about 17,000 feet and the climate would have been inhospitable very soon following the flood. At the altitude where the ark landed, the temperature would have begun to drop quickly and snow to accumulate. Noah would have likely remained on the ark for a short time due to its shelter and store of food, but he and his family would have had to descend to the valley below eventually in order to grow crops and live at a warmer climate. I suspect they made many return trips to the ark to retrieve plantings, seeds, and keepsakes before it was buried in the permanent snowcap.

It is likely that Noah and his family moved from the mountains of Ararat into the Tigris-Euphrates Valley to the south. The evidence for early population growth is greatest there. The growing numbers of Noah's descendants then began to move farther outward to replenish the earth. This outward movement began at the Tower of Babel when God confused the languages to initiate the migration of people over the surface of the earth. Population centers began first at Babel and then probably developed after the dispersion at Babylon, Ur, and Uruk.

Descendants of Noah seem to have moved primarily in three directions. Groups moved northwestward toward Europe, southwestward into Africa, and eastward into Asia. Partly from the success they had in the Tigris-Euphrates Valley and partly from the difficulty of establishing agricultural settlements elsewhere, these immigrants seemed to select river valleys in which to begin farming. Also, the rich soil and abundant water made farming easier.

A major settlement occurred along the Nile River in Egypt very soon after the dispersion from Babel. Even when the Sahara Desert formed and spread over most of North Africa, the population of people along the Nile River was able to flourish because of the annual replenishing of the soil by flooding and the easy irrigation during the dry season. The Egyptian culture has been one of the longest and most interesting civilizations since the Genesis flood. The religious aspects of Egyptian history, embodied in the purpose of the pyramids, has fascinated people for the past several hundred years. The construction of the pyramids may have had its source in structures built in the Tigris-Euphrates Valley to worship the gods. Other groups of people moved farther south in Africa and adapted to the tropical regions, exhibiting Negroid features.

Noah's descendants who moved northwest into Europe apparently ran into a colder climate, one which rapidly grew forests. Unlike the climate in Egypt, the European climate was much colder and produced heavy precipitation. Within several hundred years after the flood, the "Ice Age" developed and permanent glaciers formed on the mountains of central Europe and along the northern coasts of Europe and Asia. The peoples who had migrated to Europe were cut off from the routes they had taken from the Mideast and were isolated to the valley floors where it was warmer. Here, life was difficult and most were forced to take refuge in caves which provided consistent warmth and protection from wild animals. The groups which migrated to the northwest appear to have adapted to the colder, cloudy climates, exhibiting Caucasian features.

The Neanderthals were one group which had migrated to the Neander Valley in Germany. The short, stocky body type, deformed bones, and heavy facial brow have led some to suggest that they were an early evolutionary form of man. An alternative explanation for these features may be the climate in which they lived and the likely long life spans soon after the flood. Their apparent dependency on meat as their primary form of diet, the lack of sunshine from living in caves, and the cloudy conditions near the edge of the permanent snowpack may have led to a vitamin deficiency resulting in rickets. This condition is well known to produce deformed bones. In addition, there is evidence that for some time after the flood, people still lived for several hundred years. Certain body features, particularly the skull and jaw continue to grow slowly and take on a thickened appearance.

The third main group of Noah's descendants migrated to the east and took up residence in the river valleys of India and China. Most of Asia was not affected strongly by the Ice Age, so migration was relatively easy from the Tigris-Euphrates Valley all the way to the Pacific

Ocean in Southeast Asia. The Silk Road was established, which permitted easy trade and culture to pass back and forth between Asia, the Mideast, and North Africa. The groups which migrated toward the east apparently adapted to this environment and exhibited Mongoloid features.

China was one of the great cultures which was formed from this group; it has existed about the same length of time as Egypt. However, some of the Mongolian immigrants were not satisfied to stop at the western edge of the Pacific Ocean, but moved on into the Americas. Apparently they were able to migrate into the New World via a land bridge which developed between Asia and North America at the time of the Ice Age.

Because thousands of feet of ice and snow were precipitated onto the continents during the Ice Age, the oceans were depleted of several hundred feet of water and shallow portions of the ocean floor were exposed. The continental shelf was exposed around all continents, causing them to be larger than they are today. For example, Florida would have been about twice as large as it is now because of the ocean's receding from today's beach line to the edge of the continental shelf by tens of miles, and in some places hundreds of miles, from where it is today. Between Asia and Alaska, across the Bering Strait, the ocean is only 200-300 feet deep. This strait was exposed as dry land and migration occurred from Asia to North America.

This migration probably took place during the Ice Age. Many of the mountains in Alaska, western Canada, and the United States would have been covered with snow and ice during this time. Peoples who were later to become known as Native Americans probably migrated along the west coast of North America, through the valleys, and to the east of the Rocky Mountains. The timing of the migrations and the paths that were taken were different as the Ice Age progressed. At first the mountains would have been covered with ice and snow, blocking passes and restricting routes. Later in the Ice Age, as the glaciers began to flow to lower elevations down the mountain valleys and permanent snow accumulated at lower elevations, fewer options were available to the immigrants.

These immigrants into the New World traveled not only into North America but also into Central and South America. Great Indian cultures developed which were isolated from Asia and the Mideast, although due to tantalizing similarities between American and Asian cultures, some have suggested contact continued even after the Ice Age ended, covering the land bridge. In South America the Inca civilization developed in the Andes Mountains and along the western coastal plain. In Mexico the Aztec civilization developed on the Yucatan Peninsula and into northern Central America. And in the southwestern United States, the Anasazi civilization developed in Arizona, Utah, Colorado, and New Mexico.

Each of these civilizations had its own distinctions, but there seems to have been considerable trade and cultural exchange among the groups. The South American Incas established good communication systems and trade routes. At one point in their culture, before the Spanish made contact, they were regularly sending runners over some 6,000 miles of foot paths to and from the remotest parts of their empire. They spanned canyons with rope bridges, built overnight "motels" along the roads, and planted and irrigated trees for travelers to pick fruit and use as shade. Although the Anasazi did not develop such elaborate "highways," they did regularly send trading parties from Arizona to California and Mexico to barter for shells, birds, and other goods.

The Aztec and Inca civilizations developed earlier and reached greater heights than the Anasazi. This was probably due to the more favorable environmental conditions the Aztecs and Incas experienced. The Anasazi culture developed in the arid Southwest, which became drier after the flood. Agriculture was difficult and became even more so.

Several distinctions marked all of these civilizations. Their descendants exhibit many of the same facial and skin features of the peoples in Asia today. Many of the architectural structures and designs are similar to those in Asia, China, and the Mideast. For example, towers similar to those constructed in the Tigris-Euphrates Valley were built in the Yucatan Peninsula by the Aztecs and in the Andes by the Incas.

In these American cultures, towers appear to have been used to worship the sun god in a way similar to some of those in the Mideast. Bodies have been found buried in a few towers in the Yucatan, similar to the use of the pyramids for burial chambers in Egypt. However, the religious activities in Central and South America seemed to have taken a very bloody turn compared to Egypt and the Tigris-Euphrates Valley. Ritual sacrifice of virgins and enemies became common. Thousands were sacrificed in the name of religion in the Americas. From time to time even the king was called upon to ritually donate blood.

Many of the designs carved into the rock which decorate the stone structures in Central and South America and woven into the fabrics used for rugs, tapestries, etc., use a blocky feature to form the shape of snakes and scowling human faces. Very similar designs are found in the architecture and fabrics of China and Japan.

Some of these features are found in the Anasazi culture of the southwestern United States. Most of these similarities appear to have been introduced later by cultural interchange, however. Their culture reached its zenith in about A.D. 1000 and it is thought that they were forced out of the Four Corners region near the Grand Canyon by about A.D. 1200 by drought or enemies.

One of the strongest distinctions of the Anasazi religious system was their belief in an origin through a sipapu.

A sipapu is a hole in the earth's surface through which the Anasazi people believed they emerged from the underworld into this present world. They illustrated this origin-myth by symbolically digging a small hole in the floor of each kiva (worship chamber) they constructed.

There are places in the American Southwest which the Anasazi hold sacred because of association with what they believe were their points of origin. None are more sacred than the Grand Canyon. This large depression in the earth's surface is viewed as a giant sipapu and they believe it is filled with spirits moving between this world and the underworld. Even today the descendants of the Anasazi, tribes such as the Hopi and Zuni, who live in New Mexico along the Rio Grande River, enter the Grand Canyon with awe and some trepidation. Most Anasazi lived on the mesas surrounding the Grand Canyon; few lived down in the canyon. The farther one goes down into the canyon, the fewer artifacts of ancient tribal activities are found.

Many of our backpack groups have come across Anasazi artifacts, and these have been of great interest to tour participants. We have always been careful not to disturb these relics and to treat them with respect. We have located numerous examples of rock art, pottery, prayer circles, hunting cairns, arrowheads, chipping stations, and granaries. But the most exciting finds occurred on two backpack trips led by Don Barber.

On the trip to Cottonwood Creek which Don led in 1990, he was accompanied by his wife, Rebecca. While exploring downstream from their camp in Cottonwood Creek, they found an old miner's cabin located above the creek floor which had been built of rock previously used by the Anasazi to construct granaries. These granaries were built into the canyon walls in overhanging crevices of the Tapeats sandstone where rain and water would not damage the winter stores. The miner's cabin had been built in the late 1800s or early 1900s by miners who were searching for copper or gold down in the canyon.

While looking around for artifacts near the miner's cabin, Rebecca stumbled across a human skullcap and leg bone. Because of the condition and location of these bones, Don and Rebecca reported them to the authorities when they returned to San Diego. The police found that the skullcap and leg bone were those of a woman hiker who had been reported missing in 1951 and had never been found. Apparently, someone had killed her and buried her body in Cottonwood Creek.

On the 1990 trip Don became fascinated with other artifacts that he found in Cottonwood Creek. While searching for more evidence of occupation, Don's backpack group explored the walls above the miner's cabin and found rock cairns placed at strategic locations up the cliffs to mark ancient Anasazi trails. A rock cairn is simply a small pile of rocks stacked in such a way that others following the same route can be guided along the easiest path. They are typically placed every 20–50 feet so that when you come to a place where it is difficult to know which way to go, you can see the next cairn at a strategic location.

Many of the rock cairns located on the walls of Cottonwood Creek appeared to mark the trails to granaries. Most of these trails were no longer passable from below because of rock falls and the collapse of ledges. Some appeared to be accessible only from above and yet others probably required the dexterity of ancient Indian climbers. Don and his party were unable to explore all of these intriguing leads, but discussed them extensively in camp each night.

At the end of the week, on the way out of the canyon, Don's party decided to continue their search for evidence of the presence of Anasazi on the top of Horseshoe Mesa. They had found a few arrowheads in Cottonwood

Creek and had raised the question about how and where the Anasazi would have made them. Don suggested that the task of making arrowheads would require hours of sedentary work in a single location. These locations are called chipping stations because when numerous arrowheads are made at a single site, chips of rock remain and accumulate in piles after breaking off small pieces of flint to form the arrow's sharp tip.

Don's group searched the top of Horseshoe Mesa and found at least one chipping station. Although the Anasazi had been long gone and the tools they may have used were no longer present, Don suggested that one of the implements they most likely used to chip the edges of the arrowheads was the antler of a deer or antelope. Antlers have sharp points which would have allowed an Anasazi hunter to precisely press the edge of a thin piece of flint, chipping off small pieces until the distinctive arrowhead took shape.

As his party stood around one such potential chipping site, Don was reciting the likely scenario of an Anasazi arrowhead chipper selecting this location because of his desire to have a view of the canyon while he worked. He was describing the use of an antelope or deer antler when one of the group objected to the story because he had not seen any deer or antelope. Many deer live up on the south rim but few are seen down in the canyon. Without deer and antelope there would not be any antlers for the hunter to use in chipping his arrowheads. Before Don could respond, one of the others in the group held up an object he had just found and asked if it could have been used as a tool. Don took the object and immediately recognized it as a deer antler. The entire group suddenly felt that the hypothetical scene of an ancient Indian hunter bent over, chipping arrowheads, had become reality before their eyes!

The next year Don again led a backpack group to

Don Barber scooping away sand from an Indian burial basket in Cottonwood Creek.

Cottonwood Creek and this time prepared his group from the beginning to be on the lookout for Native American artifacts. While exploring the lower reaches of Cottonwood Creek, Don's group concentrated on the foot of the Tapeats sandstone walls above the canyon floor. Seasonal floods along the canyon floor would have removed any artifacts there. However, above the flood plain ancient artifacts are more likely. Don's group found many pottery shards, cairns, and rock paintings.

In one large rock amphitheater about 100 feet above the valley floor, Don's group made their most significant discovery. Below an overhanging wall where several rock ledges had fallen, one of Don's group sat on what appeared to be a sandy mound. While eating his lunch he noticed that the mound seemed to be caving in somewhat and appeared hollow. As he scooped away some of the sand to investigate, he noticed a fabric-like material woven out of reeds. Don was called over to look and immediately recognized the woven material as a woven Indian basket.

As the remainder of the group stood watching, Don gently scooped away more sand and uncovered the top of a basket with the lid slightly ajar. As more sand was removed, it became apparent that this was a large reed basket about three feet high and about two feet in diameter. Upon removing the lid, the top of a skull could be seen inside. Don's party had uncovered an Anasazi burial basket! Inside the basket the body had been carefully placed in the fetal position, with arms folded around the knees and head forward.

This was an incredible find! No one expected to see such an artifact. It was later determined that of all the artifacts ever found in the Grand Canyon, this was the only burial basket found below the rim. Evidences of Anasazi occupation in upper Grand Canyon are common, particularly in caves in the redwall limestone, but not burial baskets in the lower part of the canyon.

The group took many photographs of the basket and its location. They attempted to find others along the same wall. Pottery shards and granaries were found in this location, but no other burial baskets.

Before returning to San Diego, Don called the National Park Service officials and told them of the find. They were astonished and, at first, skeptical. However, when Don told them of the exact location and the care they had taken to protect the discovery, they decided to send a group of rangers to investigate. Upon confirming Don's story, they informed the chief of the Hopi tribe, who decided that the basket should remain undisturbed in the canyon. The Hopi and Zuni tribes are considered descendants of the Anasazi, not the Navajo tribe. The park service marked the basket with a metal tag which officially documents the find and carefully covered it again so that future backpackers would not encounter it. However, because our group discovered the basket, we know where it is located. Each time we take a group to Cottonwood Creek, we carefully uncover the lid for the group to see inside and then recover it again.

One other find of Anasazi artifacts in the canyon merits a brief discussion. On the Tonto Platform, at the northeastern tip of the horseshoe below Horseshoe Mesa, lie four giant rock structures which seem to defy explanation. During several rendezvous between the Cottonwood Creek and Hance Creek hiking groups over the years, I have studied these large piles of rock located about a thousand feet apart, all at the same elevation, just above the Inner Gorge.

These "cairns" are made of rectangular pieces of rock about one to three feet long, six inches thick, and six inches wide. They are stacked about six feet high and are about five feet in diameter at the base, decreasing in diameter to a single rock at the top. They are partially hollow inside. One of them has toppled over. The rocks composing the "cairns" are coated with very dark desert varnish, implying that they have been in position for hundreds of years.

Above the location of these cairns, on a ridge that runs out to a point overlooking the Inner Gorge, is a flat circle with rocks positioned at compass points. It may have been a prayer circle, although it may also have been created by backpackers in recent years, because it is not far off the Tonto Trail. However, heavy desert varnish on the surface also points to a long period of time since it was built.

Walter Barnhart has reported that there are several other circles in the canyon, one near Elves Chasm in western Grand Canyon. He believes the circles and lines drawn through the giant cairns are aligned with the sun's winter solstice. There are other sites related to the solstice nearby in the Southwest, such as at Zion Canyon. It is thought that the lines and strange patterns on the desert floor of the Nazca Valley in Peru are aligned with the summer and winter solstices and served as giant astronomical calendars. Possibly the influence throughout the Indian cultures of the Americas are reflected in the Grand Canyon as well.

One other explanation for the cairns is as totems for Anasazi hunters. It was common for Anasazi hunters to build small stacks of rocks and place a bent-twig deer as a symbol inside for good luck in hunting. However, the cairns near Horseshoe Mesa are large. If they were used for this purpose, the game the hunters were looking for must have been gigantic! It is clear that we don't really know what the purpose of these artifacts was. If you ever hike this part of the canyon and find an explanation for these giant rock cairns and circles, please let me know.

Finding artifacts like arrowheads, paintings, and the burial basket in the Grand Canyon makes the reality of ancient Indians in the canyon come alive. When camping and hiking in the bottom of this spectacular gorge, it is sometimes hard to recognize that people actually lived there, eking out a living in this desolate landscape. Although it is beautiful, it can also be a harsh environment. If you attempted to live there all year round, and raise a family of young children exposed to the elements, the heat in summer and the cold in winter would have been hard to endure. With my high-tech Gortex coat and tent, my propane stove, and my concentrated backpack food, I can survive easily for a week or so in the canyon. But, would I be able to live there for extended periods as the Anasazi did?

Thinking of the Anasazi in the Grand Canyon also reminds me of the need to get the Good News of Christ's birth, sacrificial death, and glorious resurrection to all the world. This includes the scattered tribes who still need to hear the message. We have not yet completed the Great Commission to all the world. The Anasazi who lived in the Southwest were only part of a great host of humanity which spread across the globe following the dispersion from the Tower of Babel. Experiencing firsthand the evidence for a group of people who were isolated from the rest of mankind and may have never heard the Word, convicts my heart to be more involved in world missions. We need to care more about tribes who exist today but who yet need the gospel.

THE PEOPLE OF THE BLUE-GREEN WATER

WHEN WE BEGAN TO take dozens of people at a time to the Grand Canyon we needed additional leaders who were familiar with the canyon to assist on various parts of the tour. For a few years we scheduled up to four backpacking groups of 16 members each, two busloads of up to 55 members each, and a raft group of some 35. At least one year we took almost 200 people on a tour of the canyon.

We attempted to provide 2 leaders on each backpacking group, at least 2 leaders per bus, and 1 leader for each of three rafts. This meant that we needed at least 15 leaders for some of our larger tour groups. Even using all of our professional and some support staff meant we did not have enough leaders to cover all of the needed areas.

A good tour leader must have several important qualifications to serve on a tour. A leader must, first of all, be a spiritual person capable of overseeing a small group of people in an environment which is sometimes unforgiving and dangerous. He must be able to inspire confidence in the group and make good decisions quickly. Sometimes he will be called upon to provide first aid or arrange for medical attention. He must have knowledge of one or more areas in biblical and scientific creationism, especially as applied to the Grand Canyon. He must have social skills and be able to help the group interact as a team. Safety skills are of most value in the backpacking groups but are important on the bus and rafts as well.

Since 1987 the following staff have participated in leading one or more tours to the Grand Canyon:

Gerald Aardsma, Ph.D.
Steve Austin, Ph.D.
Donald Barber, B.S.
Richard Bliss, Ph.D.
Kenneth Cumming, Ph.D.
Duane Gish, Ph.D.
Ken Ham, Dip. Ed.
Bill Hoesch, B.S.
Mark Looy, M.S.
Thomas Manning, B.S.
David McQueen, M.S.
Henry M. Morris, Ph.D.
John Morris, Ph.D.
Gary Parker, Ph.D.
John Rajca, B.S.
Larry Vardiman, Ph.D.

To augment our staff we have drawn on the willing services of many friends and associates to help lead some of the groups. The following adjuncts have assisted in leading one or more tours to the Grand Canyon since 1987:

Walter Barnhart, M.S.
Jeffrey Bones, M.S.
Van Burbach, Ph.D.
James Cooke, M.S.
David Coppedge, B.S.
Russell Humphreys, Ph.D.
John Meyer, Ph.D.
David Nutting, M.S.
Mary Jo Nutting, M.S.
Scott Rugg, M.S.
David Rush, M.S.
Hanna Rush, M.S.
Ted Seaman, M.S.
Andrew Snelling, Ph.D.
Bill Spear, D.V.M.
Kurt Wise, Ph.D.

Six of these adjunct leaders are graduates of the ICR Graduate School and contributed significantly to the efficiency with which our tours operated. David and Mary Jo Nutting have been of special assistance. They were two of the earliest graduates and have participated in more tours to the canyon than any other leader except some of the full-time faculty. David and Mary Jo always lead one of the backpacking groups as a team when they participate and have experienced some of the most rugged hiking trips on our tours. It seems that when they agree to lead a group, many times they either get stuck with the longest, driest hike or they have some event or hiker which complicates their trip.

For example, in 1995, one month before we were to conduct our tour to the Grand Canyon, the park service canceled two of our trail permits. A few weeks earlier, rain had washed out parts of two trails which we were to use and had broken the water main running from the north rim, reducing water supplies in the park. Because over 20 guests, some from overseas, had made plans and had purchased non-refundable airline tickets to join our tour, we felt it necessary to arrange for a suitable substitute trip into the canyon. One of the canceled groups was to be lead by David and Mary Jo Nutting.

For many years we had heard of stories of hikers traveling into the Havasu Canyon outside and west of Grand Canyon National Park. This canyon is the home of the Havasupai Indian Tribe and is known for the beautiful pools of blue-green water which cascade down the canyon to the Colorado River. The name "Havasupai" means "people of the blue-green water." The water emerges from an underground river flowing through the redwall limestone just above their village. It exhibits a blue-green appearance from the dissolved calcium carbonate it acquires during passage through the limestone. Upon exiting the cool underground caverns, the water warms in the summer and precipitates limestone which forms beautiful pools for swimming.

We were able to reserve camping space for our two backpacking groups in the Havasupai Indian Reservation. All guests who had originally planned to hike the main sections of Grand Canyon National Park on the canceled trails agreed to the change in plans and showed up for our tour. Unfortunately, neither David or Mary Jo Nutting nor any of our other leaders had ever hiked the Havasu Canyon. One principle we have developed over the years is to always have at least one leader in a backpacking group who has hiked the trail before. Consequently, we needed to locate someone who could join our group at the last minute and knew the trail.

David Coppedge, a highly experienced hiker and creationist speaker from the San Fernando Valley north of

Hikers enjoying swimming in Havasu Falls.

Los Angeles, agreed to join our tour and be our primary guide into Havasu Canyon. David has lead "Creation Safaris" to many places in the western United States including Yellowstone and the Grand Canyon. He had hiked the Havasu Canyon many times and willingly agreed to lead the group that year. David and Mary Jo Nutting, James Cooke, and David Coppedge became the leaders for this joint venture in 1995.

Several interesting events occurred during this particular tour. Several of the backpackers decided that rather than carrying their backpacks down to the campsite some ten miles from the trail head, they would pay the Havasupai Indians to pack them on horseback. Some even rode horses into camp. Unknown to us at the time, the Havasupai tribe commonly provide transportation down and back up the Havasu Canyon Trail. Since the Havasupai Indian Reservation is outside the National Park boundaries, the tribe has the right to regulate the use of horses and vehicles as they see fit. In fact, one of the members of our group badly sprained his ankle shortly after leaving the trail head and was able to rejoin the group later at the campsite after flying in by helicopter. Although none of the group took advantage of the opportunity, the little Indian village of Supai has a motel and a church. Some did purchase supplies at the grocery store.

Although Havasu Canyon is not as isolated or remote from conveniences as most places down the trails of Grand Canyon National Park, it has its own distinctive beauty and challenges. On several days the hiking group traveled downstream to beautiful Havasu and Mooney Falls for a swim. One day most of the group hiked all the way to the Colorado River, about ten miles downstream from the village. I was not prepared for the incredible pictures and stories which came back from this trip. Several miles below the village of Supai the river drops over cliffs of several hundred feet. The Havasupai tribe has installed metal chains in the cliffs along the trail to reduce the likelihood of hikers falling and hurting themselves. However, the views portrayed in the photographs and videos taken during this trek appeared extremely dangerous.

We are reluctant to ever send another group into this canyon because of the potential liability. However, there is the lure of stories told by this group and the rafters who hike up from below about beautiful pools of water surrounded by ferns. Some in the group apparently dove from rocks and ledges above these pools 30 feet or more into grottos below. This siren call of beautiful pools in the wilderness urges me to consider making the trip myself someday. My old hiking buddy, Dan Iles from northern California, will probably call me up someday when he reads this section and try to coerce me into taking one more trip into the canyon.

Although David and Mary Jo Nutting seem to have frequently been assigned some of the more difficult trails during our years in the canyon, they always seem to return with some of the best experiences each year. I never heard them or any of the group that went to Havasu Canyon complain about the trip. In fact, just the opposite was apparently true. It seems that this substitute trip more than sufficiently made up for the change in plans from the Bright Angel Trail in the park.

EPILOGUE

THE GRAND CANYON IS a special place. I have now been privileged to make over a dozen trips to the canyon. I have seen vistas and experienced smells and sounds that I will remember the rest of my life. I have shared in some of the sweetest fellowship this side of heaven with small groups of Christians in the Grand Canyon.

Each year when I leave the canyon after more than a week of heavy exertion, I commonly exclaim that this will be my last year. I won't be back. It's such hard work to hike the canyon. Why do I do it? But invariably the next spring I begin to sense this strange urge to visit the canyon. I have begun to relate to Zane Grey's story, *The Call of the Canyon*, in which his characters can't bear to leave Oak Creek Canyon once they've fully experienced it. The attraction of the Grand Canyon is similar and seems almost masochistic.

But the Grand Canyon is much more than a physical and emotional experience. It is also an intellectual and spiritual experience. God has provided one place on the earth where you can see almost a mile of lithified sediments stacked vertically one on top of another. You don't need years of training as a geologist to see the evidence for the Genesis flood here. By carrying your Bible in one hand and your walking stick in the other, you can understand clearly what God is telling you about earth history in Genesis 6-9. This is a "slice through earth's graveyard." "The remnants of dead things, buried by water, all over the Earth" cry out for an explanation. The explanation is given in Scripture, if one has the ears to hear.

> Knowing this first, that there shall come in the last days scoffers, walking after their own lusts, And saying, Where is the promise of his coming? for since the fathers fell asleep, all things continue as they were from the beginning of the creation. For this they willingly are ignorant of, that by the word of God the heavens were of old, and the earth standing out of the water and in the water: Whereby the world that then was, being overflowed with water perished: But the heavens and the earth, which are now, by the same word are kept in store, reserved unto fire against the day of judgment and perdition of ungodly men. But, beloved, be not ignorant of this one thing, that one day is with the Lord as a thousand years, and a thousand years as one day. The Lord is not slack concerning his promise, as some men count slackness; but is long-suffering to us-ward, not willing that any should perish, but that all should come to repentance (2 Pet. 3:3-9;KJV).

If there is any place on earth that will force us to recognize that God has brought judgment upon sin, it is at the Grand Canyon. It is not enough to simply recognize that fact, however. We must apply this truth to our own lives. We must repent of our own sins and accept God's free offer of salvation to all who ask. The remedy is simply expressed. "That if thou shalt confess with thy mouth the Lord Jesus and shalt believe in thine heart that God hath raised him from the dead, thou shalt be saved" (Rom. 10:9;KJV).

I've enjoyed sharing with you my experiences at the Grand Canyon. But this book has a much more important purpose than simply relating the fun of backpacking, rafting, or touring the canyon by bus. The underlying purpose is to help you, the reader, gain an entirely new perspective on earth history. Because of this new perspective, you should have greater confidence in the Bible and, because of this confidence come to the point where you must deal with your sin and accept God's offer of forgiveness. If you haven't come to the point in your life where you have asked God to save your soul through the finished work of Christ on the cross, I urge you to do so now. May God grant you peace, love, and joy.

Index

G

H

I

L

M

N

O

P

R

S

T

V

W

ABOUT THE AUTHOR

Dr. Vardiman has conducted research for the U.S. Air Force, Colorado State University, the Department of the Interior, and the Institute for Creation Research in the field of cloud physics and climate change for 35 years. He has taught physics and meteorology at Christian Heritage College, San Diego State University, and the Institute for Creation Research for almost 20 years of that time. Dr. Vardiman has written over 30 technical articles and 3 monographs in the field of atmospheric science. This is his first attempt at writing a popular book about his second love, backpacking the Grand Canyon.